URBAN GROWTH
& ECONOMICS

URBAN GROWTH & ECONOMICS

THOMAS W. SHAFER

Professor, Real Estate and Business Mathematics
San Diego City College

RESTON PUBLISHING COMPANY, INC.
A Prentice-Hall Company
Reston, Virginia

Library of Congress Cataloging in Publication Data
Shafer, Thomas W
    Urban growth and economics.

    Includes bibliographies and index.
    1. Urban economics. 2. Cities and towns—Growth.
3. Urbanization. I. Title.
HT321.S52   330.9'173'2   76-55781
ISBN 0-87909-853-8

© 1977 by Reston Publishing Company, Inc.
A Prentice-Hall Company
Reston, Virginia 22090

1 3 5 7 9 10 8 6 4 2

PRINTED IN THE UNITED STATES OF AMERICA

To
Tom, Rita, and Kitrina

TABLE OF CONTENTS

LIST OF FIGURES

INTRODUCTION

The United States has nearly 70 percent of its population stacked and housed together on less than one and one-half percent of the total land area in the nation. If this is a preferable mode of behavior, or if it is not, what are the compelling forces that result in such a behavior pattern on the part of the human species? Such close association between human beings and societies is not unique to the United States but rather has occurred, is occurring, or shows tendencies of occurring throughout the known world.

The ills endured by city dwellers and citizens alike because of the complexities and costs of urbanization are currently coming to the attention of most of us. Each time that we drive or walk in a crowded street, hear or read of another crime or catastrophy, pay our "public services" bills, pay our taxes, or leave the sanctuary of our homes, we are challenged to reconcile the situation within which we find ourselves.

It was provocation of this kind that has led me in the direction of the present work. Why were cities where they were? Indeed, why did cities exist at all? What determined city life and urbanization as the predominant role within which mankind must find itself? Why did some cities grow, and others of apparently the same physical advantages decline? In spite of all the apparent ill effects associated with urbanization, and the well researched warnings of scientists of every gender, the life of the average citizen of most developed countries, the life of aspiration on the part of most citizens of less developed countries continues to be that of a modern inhabitant of the metropolis.

The recurrent theme throughout this book is the association between urbanization and economic advantages. Although it is not an attempt, on my part, to prove with absolute precision that cities and urban areas are always based on exact economic benefits, and that economic advantages are the sole reason for the existence of urbanization, it is my hope to show the fragments of relationships between densities of population and the economic advantages that arise from such densities.

Part One of the text will be devoted to the historical record of urbanization and the birth and development of cities. We shall examine the similarities as well as the differences between ancient cities and those of the Industrial Revolution.

In Part Two, attention will be focused on the concept of growth and the various definitions of that term which are frequently used. We will examine the term and its elements as well as the dynamics that surround the concept of growth. This part of the text will attempt to define the concept of growth in a pragmatic sense and a usable definition in the further analysis contained.

In Part Three, chapters relate to the definition of growth and urbanization based on the use of land and land resources. We will also discuss the various theories of land use, and the social and political doctrines surrounding them. Further, the various controls over the use of land will be explored and defined in terms of their current or implied economic impact on the economics of land use and the economic factors in the functioning of urbanized areas.

Part Four examines the special role of institutions in the functioning of the market forces in relation to land use. These institutions also drastically affect the alternatives available in determining how to use land resources, those of the governmental sector and including all levels of federal, state, and local governments as well as institutions of the private sector, such as banking and finance, education, and the investment communities.

The last chapter examines some of the current trends, and indicators of future trends which are affecting and will affect the way we use real property in this increasingly urbanized world. Some of the economic assumptions underlying current trends will also be discussed.

Finally there is an Appendix for reference to more narrow subjects of concern in the urban growth area. The manner and characteristics of the production process in the land use area, and the level of production and output historically in the production area, are contained within this Appendix.

URBAN GROWTH
& ECONOMICS

HISTORY OF URBANIZATION

The beginning of text on the urbanization process logically starts with the origin and history of this phenomenon. The first permanent settlements by the human race, as well as the apparent underlying causes of such settlement, and the gradual progression in size and detail of urban settlements, are discussed along with the growth in such a trend over a large part of the world. The arrival of extensive and fully integrated empires can be traced in terms of origin in terms of cause, as well as the economic factors responsible for such empires to continue.

The second chapter focuses on the urbanization process that occurred after the beginning of the Christian Era. The characteristics which led to the "dark" Middle Ages and their economic impact, and the movement into the Industrial Revolution is then discussed along with the historical basis on which it depended. Also examined are the economic forces involved in the Industrial Revolution as well as its impact on urbanization patterns as a result of such forces.

CHAPTER ONE

ANCIENT HISTORY OF URBAN GROWTH

OUTLINE

In examining the history of the human race and man's evolvement into the city dweller we must first establish some fundamental parameters. First, there is the subject of physical evidence and the physical evolution of the human race. The history of the human being is far longer than the history of urban or city-dwelling man. This is not to say that mankind did not have the ability or capacity to become city dwellers 30,000 years ago, but is merely an observation that there is no evidence to support the contention that man was a city dweller at that time.

Much like an infant, mankind had physically developed to the point of having all the necessary physical traits to form a civilized society; but the development process is severely retarded or slowed down when there are no examples to follow or copy. When nearly every aspect of one's life has to be invented by that person, then the gestation period between having the physical tools and obtaining the skills to use those tools is stretched out over many more years.

Thus when we discover some ancient remains of a cluster of dwellings with some common defensive wall, we can reasonably deduce that the peoples that had lived there had the mental and physical skills to build a village or town long before that first town was built. What this means is that the agricultural revolution dictating urban life style most probably occurred long before the first urban community was developed. The urban way of life, as opposed to the nomadic life style, was not an independent choice made by mankind. The human experience has been and continues to be dictated by the larger external factors, such as food resources, climate, and energy resources. The cultures of the human race will generally tend to reflect those external factors. This is particularly true of the more ancient cultures and societies.

PHYSICAL EVIDENCE

The second limitation in the study of ancient peoples and their trend toward urbanization is the lack of physical evidence. The available physical evidence represents a rather sophisticated degree of construction that must have taken some time for mankind to develop. The earliest attempts at urbanization or city dwelling must have taken the form of something similar to the life style brought from the nomadic way of life. As such, most evidence that did exist quickly deteriorated and left nothing to observe centuries later.

All that can be said is that mankind probably began living in close association with others about the same time that agriculture began to be the major activity of early man. Furthermore, because so much of the world has not been searched for prehistory civilizations, we have little knowledge as to the approximate time that the human race began developing permanent urban centers.

Let us now turn to the earliest evidence of the birth of city life, and look at the early prehistoric cities and cultures that developed.

THE BIRTH OF CITIES

PRE-CITY LIFE

Cro-Magnon man lived nearly 35,000 years ago, and lived in caves in parts of Europe over 25,000 years ago. Such evidence as the cave paintings of southern France, and Spain, attests to the development of the human form as of this date. However, the evidence that exists also indicates that the populations were hunters and nomads and did not establish permanent places of living. In the pursuit of animal prey, these peoples were forced to wander and hunt as the seasons and animal herds moved about.

This is not to say that these peoples did not have the mental ability to become urbanized, but rather that their existence was dependent on the ability to pursue their primary source of food. Such pursuit made established culture in the form of permanent dwellings and nonutilitarian items wholly impossible.

Gradually the descendants of these peoples began to harvest vegetation and grain. As the dependence on vegetation began to grow, the ability to cultivate and improve the harvest of such agricultural items also began to develop.

THE EARLIEST CITIES

With the change in life pattern from nomad hunters to agriculture, the need to establish permanent dwellings was formed. Agriculture requires that the attendant watch and nurse his growing food source. Under those conditions, the earliest forms of permanent dwellings and villages began to develop. The primary cause of such a change in the life pattern on the part of the earliest man was the shift into agriculture. That is one of the major reasons why it has often been called the "agricultural revolution." It introduced a revolutionary life style that was a complete contradiction to that known by mankind for thousands of years before. It was also completely different from anything observable in nature by those same primitive peoples. It is not so surprising to find man in basically his present form on the earth for nearly 20,000 years before he developed the knowledge, insight, or had divine luck to become a primitive farmer.

With the development of agriculture came the need for small groups of people to associate together so that implements and mutual defense and exchange of knowledge could be had by all. The major threat in the earliest stages was the threat of invasion and looting by the nomadic tribes which still constituted the majority of human populations. The basic characteristic of agriculture is that the harvest is once or twice a year, and therefore the quantity must be stored for the period between harvests. The accumulation of foodstuffs was a tempting attraction for nomadic hunters that prevailed at this time in the history of man.

THE OLDEST CITY

Since the earliest settlements had to be small by the nature of the world and human development at the outset of the agricultural revolution, as yet there is little or no evidence found of these earliest of human settlements.

That raiding nomads did in fact constitute a viable threat to the farmer is evidenced by the remains of the oldest city on record. The town of Jericho has shown to contain a wall of defense dating back to nearly 7000 B.C. Although only a fairly large town could afford the time and material and labor commitment involved in such a formidable defense, it surely is evidence that with the growth of agricultural sectors the settlements were indeed making steady progress nearly 9,000 years ago.

THE FERTILE CRESCENT

There is an area in the Middle East that contains the oldest cities yet to be found. Jericho is one of them; Babylon, Ur, and several other ancient cities are to be found in the same area. That area is known as the Fertile Crescent. As ancient man began to roam out of Africa and the European continent, he found the Fertile Crescent. The area is of some geological interest because of the mountain ranges and seas which have cut it apart from the other areas. It is thought that such geological activity accounted for the entrapment of this alluvial plain, and the resultant fertile land contained in this former lakebed. This land is unusually fertile as compared to lands of northern Africa and the East. Crops could be easily cultivated to support an indigenous population. It is in this crescent-shaped area that the oldest cities and cultures are found. It is also this area that has seen the most powerful societies grow, and has also seen the periodic conquering and occupation which continue to the present day.

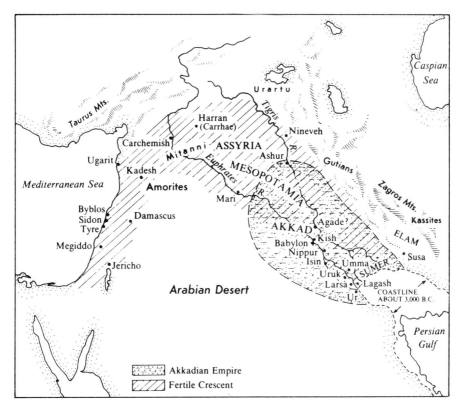

Figure 1-1 *Mesopotamia 3000 B.C.*

Source: Thomas W. Africa, *The Ancient World.* (Boston: Houghton Mifflin Co., 1969) p. 8. Reprinted by permission of the publisher.

The Sumerians of the area surrounding Babylonia established a large and rather developed culture around 5000 B.C. In
the part called Sumer, there were founded city-kingdoms. The
advent of a permanent population led to the establishment of
religious leaders and chieftains. The culture of Sumer was
founded on the agriculture base enhanced by the containment of
water and irrigation of the land for crops. Through this agricultural base, surpluses developed which could be used in trade
with the nomadic peoples of the area and other communities
which became established by this time.

With all the trading and development, the advent of a
written language was not to be denied much longer. Indeed, it

was in this same culture that the first written language in stone and clay was found. Nearly all the evidence found to date has been recordings concerning trade and storage of goods within the Sumerian culture.

Further evidence of the rather advanced state of urbanization represented by the ancient cities of the Fertile Crescent is the oldest large city in the world. The city of Uruk, which became prominent around 2700 B.C., at that time had a population of nearly 50,000. The city was surrounded by a defensive perimeter, much as the city of Jericho. To defend and support the population, the economic advantages of cultivating the land and becoming adept at trading had to be refined to an extent unknown in any of the previous history of man.

From 3000 B.C. there have been many large ancient city empires; most were established on the military power to defend an area against invaders, and on the power to extort food and products from the farming population. As in most such cases, the occupation of new territory brings with it the class of labor of slaves and serfs. City-states such as Babylon, which had a population of more than 300,000; Memphis, with its pyramids and sphinx; Mareb, of structures several stories high; Crete, with its developed shipping and trade; and the large Roman and Greek empires which followed, are examples of such ancient city formation.

EMPIRE BUILDING

Although there is evidence of minor settlements inhabited as far back as 7000 B.C., and perhaps some even more ancient, the first truly large urban society was most probably in Egypt. The unique location and fertile lands of the Nile led to wandering nomadic peoples settling in that area because of the steady source of food and tolerable climate. The growth of this area most likely began long before the age of the pyramids. As long ago as 4200 B.C. this society had developed the calendar which is nearly the same as the one we use today. Not long after that development the Egyptians also developed the alphabet. This was a major advance in the culture and development of thought in the history of the human race.

The structure of such an empire was based on the control

of water for the irrigation of the grain crops grown at that time. The chieftains controlled the water and irrigation systems. Through this power they were able to extract taxes in return for water. These same chieftains gained religious power in addition to the economic power they had. Thus we have an example of one of the earliest urban forms which had a complete division of labor and two distinct classes of citizens. There were the farming population, and the ruling and administering population. In addition, there grew a military class out of need to defend the growing economy from the invasions into the territory by the tribes of the nomadic deserts and of the northern and eastern mountains.

As an illustration of the extent of urbanization represented by the Egyptian Empire, stonecutting had been developed by 3000 B.C. The pyramids were built around 2900 B.C., consisting of more than 2 million limestone blocks each and were more than a ton in weight. Such a task consumed the labor of more than 100,000 workers for more than 20 years. Imagine the economic commitment involved in supporting more than 100,000 laborers and their families for a period of more than 20 years. It is highly illustrative of the extent of development represented by a people more than 5,000 years ago.

THE SUMERIAN EMPIRE

The Sumerian Empire grew out of approximately 3000 B.C. and was based on the same specializations as the Egyptian. That is, the ruling class performed the military duties and controlled and repaired the irrigation system on which the economic structure depended. Although not nearly the size of the Egyptian Empire, the Sumerian Empire was another example of a well advanced social and economic system based on the division of labor and specialization among classes.

THE BABYLONIAN EMPIRE

The kingdom of Babylon was also founded on the agricultural base of the area. The ruling class held power through religion and the temples which were the first banks of mankind. The temples provided safe storage for materials and valuables. Although coins were not as yet minted, there was a defined unit of value in gold and silver. Each unit of measure was a specified weight of gold or silver. With this unit of value established, it became possible to lend wealth. Babylonia was the first known culture to establish the custom of lending wealth for periods of time at an interest rate. The Babylonian Empire is probably best known for one of its great leaders, Hammurabi. He established a code of law, and had the laws and customs of the realm reconciled and written. That code of law is today one of our bases for common law in the United States. All this had taken place more than 4,000 years ago.

ARAMEAN EMPIRE

The Aramean kingdom developed near what is now called Damascus, which was a settlement of little significance since about 3000 B.C. In 1300 B.C. the Aramean kingdom was well established through conquests of a military nature. The major force behind the success of the kingdom was the key location of the area at a junction of trading routes in Asia Minor. Thus trading and commerce were the basic activities generating the wealth and power which enabled the kingdom to survive and prosper.

THE ASSYRIAN KINGDOM

From around 1200 B.C., until nearly 600 B.C., the Assyrian Empire flourished. The Assyrians were former nomads from the eastern portions of the Fertile Crescent. Their major city, Sargonburg, was named after their leader, Sargon. He and his armies were ruthless warriors who set about to totally annihilate the hated former occupying forces of Babylonia. In their path they laid in total ruin the city of Babylon, of which little remains of what the beautiful city once represented. The major city of Sargonburg had a population of more than 80,000 inhabitants at one time, and gave the world its first library.

The Assyrians were so ruthless in their conquests that they set their own destruction in motion as they were conquering the Fertile Crescent. In their savage revenge and conquests, the Assyrians destroyed nearly all the former industrial, commercial, and agricultural bases of the areas conquered. Afterward, the constant requirements of huge armies began to fall under their own weight from lack of a sufficient economic base to provide support.

THE CHALDEAN EMPIRE

The Chaldean Empire overthrew the Assyrians around 600 B.C., and continued until about 500 B.C. Their intent was to reestablish the city of Babylon. They succeeded to some extent, but the focus of the ruling class was on the past. In focusing on the past and the reliving of that past, they soon fell into internal decay and disintegration.

THE PERSIAN EMPIRE

The Persian Empire represents the first time that an eastern Asian people of Indo-European extraction established a true empire. The Persian Empire grew to be one of the first truly world empires. At its height the Persian Empire included all the Fertile Crescent, Asia Minor, and most of civilized parts of the Mediterranean. In effect, the Persian Empire ran from the western portion of India to the Mediterranean Sea, an area nearly the same size as the present United States. The political structure was of a provincial nature, much like our states.

Economically the Persians coined gold and silver for the first time, with gold being worth thirteen times as much as silver. They also rebuilt the Egyptian canal from the Nile River to the Red Sea for trade and commerce. Finally the Persians allowed the Jews exiled in Babylon to return to the area of Palestine from which they were exiled around 700 B.C. For nearly 300 years the Persian Empire was the center of the civilized world and commanded the economic resources and manpower from India to the Mediterranean Sea.

THE GREEK EMPIRE

The Greeks began to establish their independence from the Persians around 300 B.C. Like the Persians, the Greeks established an empire of extreme size and wealth. Also like the Persian Empire, the Greek Empire was very sophisticated in terms of organization and the development of cities within the empire. The Greek Empire represents the evolution of civilization out of the ancient world and into the world after the death

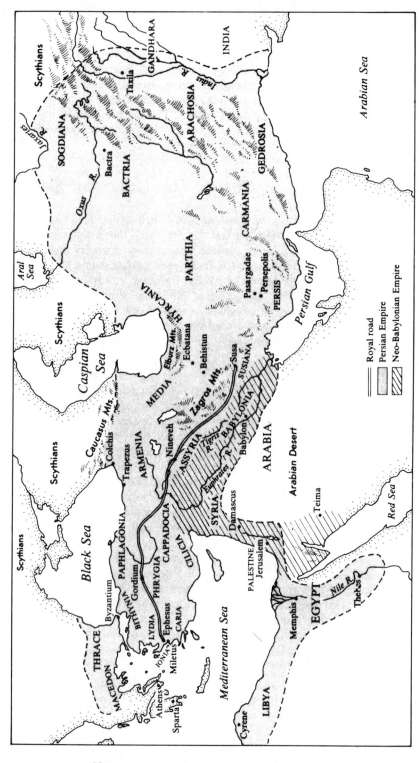

Figure 1-2 *The Persian Empire*

Source: Thomas W. Africa, *The Ancient World*. (Boston: Houghton Mifflin Co., 1969) p. 51. Reprinted by permission of the publisher.

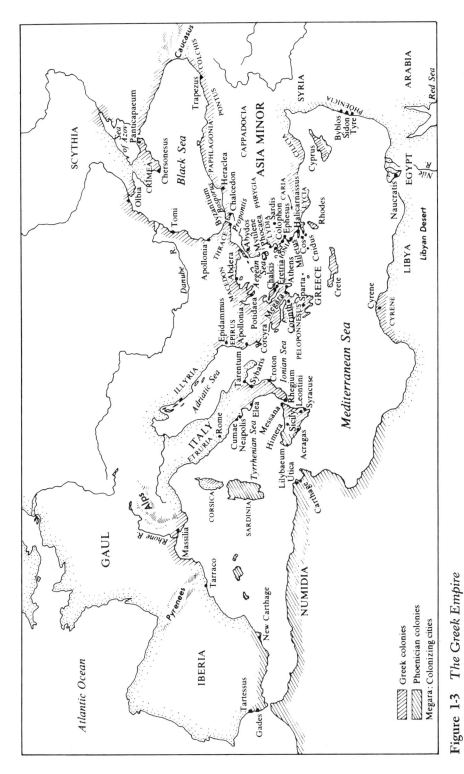

Figure 1-3 *The Greek Empire*

Source: Thomas W. Africa, *The Ancient World*. (Boston: Houghton Mifflin Co., 1969) p. 95. Reprinted by permission of the publisher.

13

of Christ. Therefore we will study the Greek Empire more closely in the following chapter on the historic cities and empires.

CIVILIZATION AND LAND USE

We have seen that civilization and using land are intimately entwined. As the nomadic life style of constant movement and migration evolved into the permanent life style of the farmer, the entire culture of mankind also began to evolve into that of an urban life style.

The earliest communities were found in unique areas containing fertile soil combined with tolerable climates which induced the prolific production of agricultural crops and vegetation. The surrounding areas around these early settlements was either arid desert, or mountainous areas providing little vegetation or fertile soils.

Urbanization represents a major shift in the human experience. From living off the animal migrations and indigenous vegetation found in the nearly constant movement of the nomadic peoples, the urban dweller cultivated his crops and remained in one place. This allowed the formation of social structure and culture, formal religious practices, and advance of knowledge available through time saved from traveling and pursuing.

The societies we have glanced at in this chapter are merely representative of the development of mankind and do not hold to restate all human development to the time of Christ. Nevertheless, there are clear indications that certain factors and trends in development were of major and nearly universal importance.

MAJOR FACTORS IN ANCIENT HISTORY

The primary influence in the birth of urbanization was the development of agriculture. Not only was agriculture the primary attraction of the nomadic peoples in their initial settling, but agriculture represented the major base of existence for the ancient urban centers in total. It was the inherent advantages of certain regions, from an agricultural point of view, that led to the ancient civilizations being founded in those very same areas.

Indeed, the Fertile Crescent and the Nile River floodplain were the very birthplace of the urbanization as we know it today. It is almost a certainty that any evidence of ancient societies to be found anywhere else in the world will surely be based on a fertile area for foodstuffs.

The second major characteristic of the ancient urban areas is the vital importance of the military. As all nomadic peoples did not become farmers at the same time, those that did form permanent living areas became highly vulnerable to the pillage by the wandering nomads of the mountains and deserts close by. Such vulnerability dictated that defensive measures had to be taken on the part of the early farming community. The ancient city of Jericho with its stone walls is but one example of this behavior.

The rise and fall of the many powerful communities during ancient history was but a natural consequence of the conflict between the nomadic life of survival and the permanent life and culture of the city dweller. In the later development of cities and empires, the power group tended to rule through force and intimidation, with nearly always one group or another being subjected to slavery or serfdom. Such extortion for the benefit of power groups merely insured the continuation of the cycle between nomadic conquerors and domestic empire building.

MEDIEVAL CITIES

THE GREEK EMPIRE

Although not properly a medieval city or empire, the Greek Empire acts as the bridge between the early development of urbanization and the later trends characterized by the medieval cities and kingdoms. The Greek Empire was the third major empire in history, after the age of Egypt and the Persian empires. Its cities tended to be large and well developed. Its economic base included many specialized areas, such as textiles and manufacturing of various kinds. Also, there existed a massive administration and aristocratic layer of the population in addition to the merchants and laborers.

The development of the Greek Empire is somewhat repre-

sented by the city of Rhodes, which attained a population estimated to near 100,000. In addition, the establishment of the
arts and culture were brought to a new height in the Greek
Empire. The role of education in reading and writing was established in the Greek Empire to such an extent that children of
the upper social and economic classes were expected to be literate for the first time in the cultural evolution of the human
species. Arts, music, poetry, and organized festivals were a major
part of Greek society.

The structure of the Empire was based on the military
dominion over many communities and tribal groups. Under such
control, these sectors of the developed world at that time were
compelled to pay taxes and support the burdensome upper
classes. Trading, commerce, and, of course, agriculture were the
major sectors of the economic base of the Greek Empire.
Through the control over vast territories, special advantages of
each were able to be integrated with the complement advantages
of other areas within the empire for natural trading and commerce.

As a result of the coordination that was possible when such
diverse areas were under one governmental structure, the growth
of trading and commerce was such as had not been witnessed in
the long history of civilized man to this point in history.

ECONOMIES OF SCALE

The mere size of the Greek Empire allowed the division of labor
to be carried to a point previously unknown in urban man. As a
result of such segmentation of the population into specialized
pockets, the skills and accomplishments of each sector advanced
rapidly.

The growth of the economic and agricultural sectors gave
rise to the accumulation of wealth and the subsequent investment in manufacturing, trading, and commercialism. The gain
on the part of the nation was also the accumulation of wealth,
which allowed the maintaining of large standing defenses and
the development of society on a scale never before seen in
human history. The growth of art, architecture, sculpture, painting, and the development of education in the sciences and arts
as well as philosophy truly represent a major threshold in the
development of man.

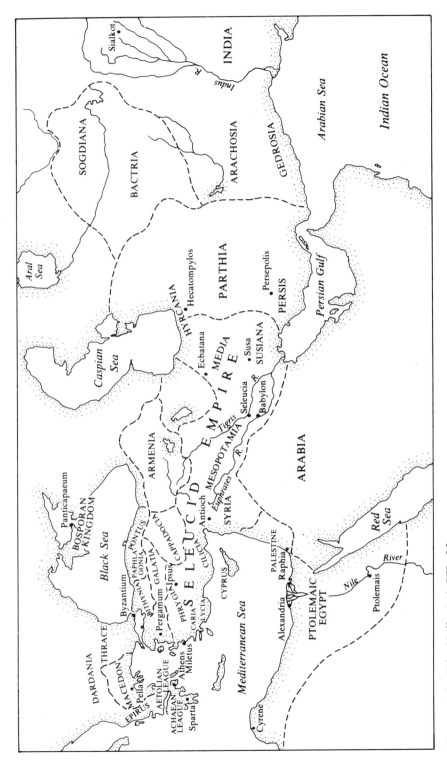

Figure 1-4 *The Hellenistic World*

Source: Thomas W. Africa, *The Ancient World*. (Boston: Houghton Mifflin Co, 1969) p. 235. Reprinted by permission of the publisher.

This scale of refinement is probably nowhere more exemplified than in the city of Alexandria and its lighthouse, which rises more than 30 stories and has survived for more than 2,000 years. Such a structure also illustrates the importance of trade and commerce rather than just religious and/or military dominance.

FALL OF THE GREEK EMPIRE

The Greek Empire was so large, and the administrative structure so immature, that the entire empire slipped into many separate city-states each with its own self-interest at heart. Other factors such as mercenary troops, despotic leadership, and the high cost of continuing military actions in all directions soon proved too much for the Greeks to endure as a nation. It did not collapse in one moment, but rather led to a steady decline. During this decline, other nations and powers began to gain a position in the world of civilized and cultured mankind.

THE ROMAN EMPIRE

As the Greek Empire began to decline into the many city-states, and its military defenses began to wane, the city-state of Rome began to assert itself. The birth of the Roman Empire was around the year 80 B.C., and was almost entirely based on military power. The contrast between the bloody spectacles of gladiators in Rome and the refined culture of music and dance of the Greeks, shows the basic reasons for the success of the Roman Empire.

Through pure military aggression, the Roman Empire was able to establish itself. Once the Roman power structure was established, the operation of the cities under control was much in the same manner as before the Romans; that is, the economic specialty of each area remained essentially unchanged from the previous dominance of the Greeks.

Because essentially the Romans were military and lacked much of a cultural base, they tended to incorporate and duplicate the arts and culture of the Greeks. There was much sacking of former Greek and Hellenistic cities and the transport of the art and sculpture back to Rome and other cities of the Italian peninsula. What is important to note is that at the height of

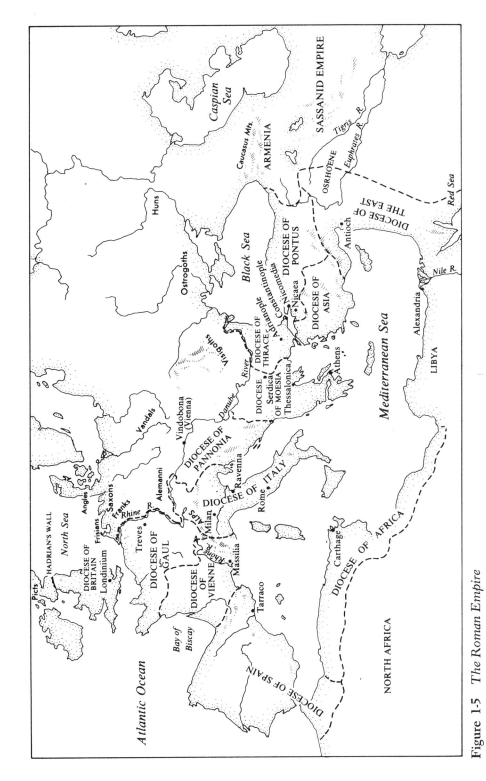

Figure 1-5 *The Roman Empire*

Source: Thomas W. Africa, *The Ancient World.* (Boston: Houghton Mifflin Co., 1969) p. 475. Reprinted by permission of the publisher.

the Roman Empire, as many Romans were literate in Greek as they were literate in the Latin language.

The Roman Empire was largely based on the military power of the nation, and on the efficiency with which the Romans conducted trade and commerce. Although the religious position of the ruler was at times very high, the presence of the military and the advantages of trade were always present. The importance of these factors is aptly illustrated in the size of the Roman Empire at its zenith. The Roman Empire included nearly all lands from Asia Minor on the east, the Nile Valley on the south, the northern part of Africa to the Atlantic on the west, and extended to include the British Isles, western Europe, and parts of Germany on the north.

Through efficient banking and monetary systems, refined postal services, and efficient shipping and trading centers, the Roman Empire with large military commitments was able to survive and prosper for nearly ten centuries. That survival was not smooth and constant, but included many major struggles and changes within the power base of the empire. In fact, only two of the ten centuries were noticeably without war. The major asset in the long survival of the Roman Empire was the ability or good fortune of the nation to survive change in its major political structure.

THE DECLINE OF THE ROMAN EMPIRE

The Roman Empire did not fall suddenly or drastically as did many smaller nations before it; but, rather much like the Greek Empire, the Roman Empire began to fall under its own weight. Supporting and defending a nation as large as the Roman Empire required two major things. First, a strong and highly productive agricultural base on which the rest of the empire could survive. Second, a huge standing military to protect and enforce the policies of the central government. Both sectors deteriorated into local factions which left them and the empire vulnerable to outside attack.

The agricultural base was severely abused through the taking of able men into the military, and the abandoned lands going into the hands of the nobles appointed from Rome and

farmed by less efficient slave and serf labor. Gradually the c
tion of foodstuffs reached the point of payment for taxes be.
made in foodstuffs rather than in coin.

The decline of the military began when the empire did not
have sufficient manpower to arm all its military contingents all
over the empire. As a result, many mercenaries began to join the
major portions of the Roman army. At the outlying frontiers,
entire areas were defended by foreign troops made up of captives
from previous wars and by inhabitants of occupied towns. It was
not long thereafter that such troops were recruited by the former
barbarians to overthrow the Roman influence.

The end of the Roman Empire came in piecemeal fashion,
when tribes from various sectors began to organize and learn
from the Romans how to conduct military campaigns and hold
occupied lands. The Gauls, the Saxons, the Moors, the Huns,
the Mongols, and the Persians, all began to experience success at
taking former Roman outposts. It was not long till much of what
was formerly the Roman Empire had become separate lands and
kingdoms.

Essentially the cause of the decline of the Roman Empire
was actually the loss of control over the military and economic
bases of the empire on the part of the central governing unit.
Many additional factors also contributed to the decline, such as
the huge public spectacles, the immense corruption and bribery
of local bureaucrats, mandated holidays that forbade working
as much as more than half the total days in a year, the changes
and faction-building process of religious and spiritual dictates
which changed many times, and the gradual decay of Rome itself from the congestion and nonproductive elements of the city.

The major identification of the decline of the Roman Empire was in the changes forced on it by external rather than internal forces. These externally forced changes were mostly the
direct result of the degeneration of the economic and military
base of the empire. In spite of all the truly remarkable engineering and architectural advantages of the Roman Empire, the disadvantages endured by the outlying areas in terms of economics
and military defense were strong enough to lead to a disassoci-
ation with Rome and a new association with the newer regimes
developing along the perimeter.

The status of urbanization during medieval times greatly varied from one locality to another. After the decline of the Roman Empire, the Christian movement became prominent. As a result, the role of the new Christian Church was a prominent one. The strong commitment to establishing the new Christian thought, and the degrading of the old Roman philosophies, led to the exodus from the major Roman centers and the criticism of the literature and accomplishments of the Roman Empire.

The growth of local city-states throughout the former Roman Empire, and the growth of the Christian Church through monasteries, led to the loss of the economies of scale and the major trading activity which characterized the Roman Empire. As a result, the local areas began to form in feudal structures for the protection they offered from the raiding and war activities of the many nobles of the time. The feudal system offered security from the savage forces of the countryside, but the price of such security was serfdom and a hard caste structure offering little to the major numbers of inhabitants.

Throughout this period in history, cities lying at critical junctures in trading patterns continued to grow. For the population, as well as the nobles, had cultivated an appetite for the luxuries that trading could provide. In addition, the manufacturing facilities in many towns were continuing in their importance. Such activities on the part of the major trading cities offered a great attraction to the skilled craftsman living in some form of serfdom within the walls of some feudal lord. It was not long until many of these craftsmen made their way into the larger cities. Once there, they found employment and higher wages in addition to freedom from the former feudal lord in the country.

The development of industry began to accelerate, and the unification of the city-states under a king or prince offered some advantages over the old feudal system. The nations and states that arose were nothing like the old empires in terms of the massive bureaucracies that fed off the productive elements of the societies. Although the new church movement was born in communal effort and in contrast to the materialism of the Greek and Roman empires, the new communities were largely run and managed by the Church, and the materialism of old began to reappear.

The major difference in the cities of the Middle Ages was the three-chaired power system that developed. There were the merchants that constituted the major economic force; the Church that constituted the major philosophical and moral power; and the king or prince who was the administrative leader and military power of the community. Such diversity was in sharp contrast to the monolithic structure of the Roman and Greek civilizations.

As the cities of trade and commerce began to develop, they also began to alienate themselves from the surrounding country. As the country in surrounding areas of the cities was the major provider of foodstuffs, this division ultimately resulted in major political upheavals in the later part of the Middle Ages. The stories of Robin Hood, Sir Lancelot, and many others of that time, reflect that the conditions between the townsfolk and the country people were anything but compatible. At this time most towns were much like the walled cities of old, providing citizens with certain securities, and serving notice to all others that this community was under the control and dictate of a certain king or prince.

THE ROLE OF INDUSTRY

The position of the capitalist and merchant in the late Middle Ages grew to a stature never before realized in the development of urban life. With power divested into three different groups, each vied for its own success. This new freedom, when combined with the subtle change of allegiance from one central figure to oneself and the Church and the king, led to a stimulus to growth of personal wealth and development unsurpassed up until this time.

The development of new technology and manufacturing processes, as well as the harnessing of new energy sources, led to large-scale business enterprises. Such large-scale manufacturing had a very important impact on the development of urbanized areas at this point in human history. The cities were largely controlled by guilds of skilled workers who demanded higher wages far above those to be found outside the major cities.

It did not take long for business to react to this difference. Major manufacturing points began to form on the outskirts of major cities where adequate land and resources could support manufacturing. At the same time there were also sufficient labor pools to meet the demands of large-scale manufacturing at wage rates far below those to be found in the cities, where guilds controlled the labor pool and secured higher wages. In turn this led to the formation of manufacturing facilities and the attendant housing facilities for workers being located outside the confines of the major cities.

Originally many such cities were formed by some monarch and contained some of the elements of a formal patterned layout. With the advent of manufacturing facilities, the cities began to take on the appearance of urban sprawl, which characterizes many of the cities in the contemporary world.

What is important to note in the late Middle Ages is the evolvement of individual self-interest as the primary economic forces in the patterns of development of most cities. No longer was there a formal god and emperor who decided what form a city should take. The role of economics suddenly began to be the primary role in urbanization, as opposed to the previous role of the military and/or religion in determining the functioning and pattern of operation for centralized economic activity.

LAND USE AND CIVILIZATION

From the evidence we now have concerning the development of the human species we know that mankind first began to become a city dweller more than 10,000 years ago. Surely man began to inhabit small villages, and even temporary village sites, long before that. The knowledge we have of those early peoples is largely confined to those who were town and city dwellers. The history of the human species is essentially the history of city civilizations. The growth and development of mankind is intimately entwined with the growth and development of city civilizations.

From the earliest settlements of the Fertile Crescent to the major empires of the Persians, Egyptians, Greeks, and Romans, the role of the city and the city dweller steadily grew both in scale and the degree of sophistication. Indeed, all the major accomplishments of the human race, beyond that of mere survival and endurance, have virtually occurred within the auspices of the urban system. It is through such major advantages as those offered in the division of labor and specialization that mankind has been afforded the luxury of intellectual and cultural development. This development has been preconditioned by the more intensive use of land resources. Through the more effective agricultural and natural resource industries, mankind has been able to become a permanent dweller rather than a nomadic wanderer.

From that humble beginning, trade and division of labor and activity has led to even concentration of population into selected activities within selected areas. The progressively intense use of land for certain crops, certain resources, certain inhabitants, and certain specialized uses has paralleled the growth of the human race into civilized (as well as naive and savage) and cultured humanity.

MAJOR FACTORS OF URBANIZATION

What little we know about the very beginnings of human settlement includes only a small portion of the world. The major factor from such evidence appears to be natural foods of such a nature as to provide for the needs of humans throughout the entire year or the majority of it. Such conditions led previously nomadic and hunting peoples to establish themselves more or less permanently in one area. The importance of agriculture appears to be the most single important factor which influenced the early stages of settlement.

Another major influence in settlements of a permanent nature was the existence of trade. Where a junction in trade routes appeared, there was also a trend toward some permanent settlement. The inhabitants were able to maintain a permanent residence and support their physical needs through exchange of wanted resources, such as obsidian, soapstone, and other items, for certain foodstuffs and supplies carried by the nomadic traders of that era.

Agriculture and critical trading routes were apparently the

major initial factors leading to the first permanent settlements by mankind. It was a considerable time later, however, when either of these two activities reached such a scale that they enabled the inhabitants of those settlements to build and maintain structures of public or overall nature and to maintain such structures. The vulnerability of early settlements to the nomadic tribes and competing trading or agricultural settlements is evidenced by the first truly public or social construction for the benefit of a homogenous group of citizens being the defensive wall or buttress of the earliest cities. The scale of such construction and commitment in terms of time and labor on the part of individuals for the benefit of the overall community represents one of the major characteristics of a city or town.

The cohesiveness and administration of a settlement through some central body or person would be required for structures such as these to be built. Such organization represents a great change from the tribal or nomadic life and could be described as the beginning of the second stage of human urbanization—the first stage being the founding of unique economic advantages associated with a given local area and providing the means through which permanent residents could be physically supported on a nearly year-round basis.

As the number of groups of residents in various settlements began to increase, and the settlements themselves began to develop unique patterns of human behavior and socialization, the amount of friction between the city dwellers and the nomadic peoples, as well as the friction that began to arise between different settlements, brought about the unification of the city peoples. Initially such unification was for purposes of defense, and gradually grew to the point of offensive power and the philosophical and religious unification of various city peoples behind or in support of one ideology or another. In addition the attractive advantages of city living began to attract increasing numbers of former nomadic peoples into the city, and the growth of urban centers was also a major factor leading to the subsequent trends and patterns.

The second stage of urbanization was climaxed in the huge military conquests and domination of large areas of settlement by various peoples that were previously nomadic and hunters by nature. The Assyrians, Persians, Babylonians, and the Egyptians are examples of such large dominion primarily through military conquest and control. The major characteristics of those states were the control of major economic resources and the development of huge religious and philosophical hierarchies within the ruling class.

This period of human history is a series of military conquests and control over economically rich areas of trade and agriculture, and the decline and defeat of such states by new powers who merely repeated, to a large extent, the same military control and extortion of previous conquerors. Gradually the scale of military engagements began to reach great heights, and the areas so conquered also increased to a large size. This new scale of unification introduced another stage in the long process of human urbanization.

The Persians, the Greeks, and others developed their empires along lines fundamentally based on the economic benefits of certain areas. The importance of trade within and between various empires, as well as the accumulation of wealth to the extent of carrying on the development of the mind and the culture of an empire, seemed to characterize this third stage of urbanization.

Written language of a uniform nature throughout the empire; acceptable monetary systems to facilitate trade and commerce; the education of youth; commitment to the development of science and mathematics; and the great development of culture and the creative arts as symbolized by the Greeks in the Hellenistic age, are characteristic of this stage of development. Also, as with the Greeks, this stage of urbanization, with its development of the gentle arts of knowledge and philosophy and fine arts, led to the deemphasis of military strength, which led to the collapse of these same large urban empires.

If it is possible to view the Romans as a separate stage of urbanization, then they would be characterized as not emphasizing the finer cultural arts as did the Greeks. But in their huge empire the Romans were more concerned with military prowess, combined with capital investments in aqueducts, roads, canals, and other major social investments routed in the economic advantages which resulted from such investments. It may be viewed that the cultural and capital improvements as never before seen in the urbanization process were largely responsible for the survival of the Roman Empire for such a long period of time. The development of transportation, postal service, monetary systems, refined language and communication were at the very core of the success of the Roman Empire.

In spite of the massive public buildings of the Roman period, and the huge investment of labor, land, and capital in such activities as circuses, gladiator spectacles, and other such nonproductive activities, the economic advantages of the Roman Empire and to those within it were much greater than the available alternatives of the time. If that had not been the case, maintaining absolute control over an area larger than the current nation of the United States of America would have been all but totally impossible.

The final stage of urbanization prior to the Industrial Revolution was characterized by the disintegration of the Roman Empire into numerous smaller nations and city-states, each localized in its perspective and competing with other such states. It was, however, set on the economic blueprint of capital investments made by the Romans that such interaction among these newer city-states occurred. The roads, shipping, monetary, and architecture of the Romans were continued in use throughout much of what is now Europe and North Africa. The rise of Christianity was also a major factor in the pattern of urbanization at this time.

The role of the Church began to play a major part in the layout, operation, and growth of cities during this period. There was, however, one major new characteristic of the cities of this era. As Lewis Mumford pointed out in his book, *The City in History*, there was largely a three-chaired form of leadership at this stage in city development. There was a king or prince as monarch and in charge of war defenses and administration of the state; there was the Church and its hierarchy in charge of religion and morals of the citizenry; and then there was the merchant who ruled the world of commerce and trade in a sort of collective club fashion. This structure actually released the powerful economic forces that previously had been little understood and poorly structured and managed.

It was not long until the commercial aspects of the city-states and nations began to constitute the predominant force in terms of the urban structure and the land use of the realm. The

dictates of the profit motive led to much small-scale development and haphazard planning on the growth of cities. As before,
the former central religious figure and emperor was missing, and,
with that omission—or deletion—the role of central planning
was confined to the designing of palaces and churches rather
than entire towns. The forces so unleashed grew rapidly and
forced massive changes on the physical as well as on the political
scene and into the present day.

SELECTED READINGS

Africa, Thomas. *The Ancient World*. Boston, Mass.: Houghton
  Mifflin Co., 1969.

Brested, James H. *Ancient Times: A History of the Western World*.
  Boston, Mass.: Ginn and Company, 1916.

Bronowski, J. *The Ascent of Man*. Boston, Mass.: Little, Brown and
  Company, 1973.

Comhaire, Jean, and Werner J. Chanman. *How Cities Grew*. 4th ed.
  Florham Park, N.J.: Florham Press, 1971.

Davis, Kingsley. *Cities: Their Origin, Growth, and Human Impact*.
  San Francisco, Calif.: W. H. Freeman Company, 1973.

De Coulanges, Fustel. *The Origin of Property in Land*. London:
  Swan Sonnenschein Co., 1891.

Gibbon, Edward. *The Decline and Fall of the Roman Empire*.
  Chicago: Encyclopedia Britannica Inc., 1952.

Lopreate, Joseph. *Vilfredo Pareto*. New York: Thomas Y. Crowell
  Company, 1965.

Smith, Adam. *An Inquiry into the Nature and Causes of the Wealth
  of Nations*. Chicago: Encyclopedia Britannica Inc., 1952.

CHAPTER TWO

URBANIZATION AND INDUSTRIALIZATION

It is important to remember that the Industrial Revolution was not a single event in the history of mankind, but rather a term used to describe a sequence or flow of events which apparently began in a rather narrow time frame. The sequence of events from the very beginnings of urbanization in Mesopotamia, over 9,000 years ago, and through to the present day are events which flow rather than step from one to another. The clean breaks between one culture or civilization and another that would make their study so much more clear and simplified simply do not exist.

As one moves his study more closely to the contemporary scene, the complexities of cultures and the growth and organization of the human species over the past 10,000 years make it even more difficult to differentiate one era from another. The reason for this is that at any given time there are most likely several groups of human beings going through some stage of development as individuals or as societies that many other groups have already gone through. The so-called Industrial Revolution is much that way, in that even today there are some nations and peoples that are just moving into the age of industry and mechanization.

The success of mankind to survive and grow in population to the point of dominating the entire world, and having aspirations of continued domination into the outer worlds of space, attests to man's flexibility and adaptability. It is this tremendous growth and adaptability that largely accounts for the extreme variety in the urbanization of mankind; therefore it would be very naive to offer one type of settlement as an example for all urbanization in the world. There are as many variations as there are cultures; and the extent of urbanization is so great that cities of all sizes and descriptions are to be found everywhere.

What we intend here is to study the differences in the urbanization of the human species in association with industrialization. In other words, we now turn to the study of the impact of industrialization on the process of urbanization and the characteristics of city growth brought about and associated with the Industrial Revolution. The process of becoming an industrialized society brought with it major changes in the scale and manner of society and urban centers in particular.

PRELUDE TO THE INDUSTRIAL REVOLUTION

From the decline of the Roman Empire until the beginning of the Industrial Revolution, many events and preconditions existed that were crucial to the process of industrialization. Long after the fall of Rome, the tremendous communication systems established under the Romans continued to be important to the economies of Europe. The rise of Christianity after the fall of Rome also led to some important social and philosophical preconditions which helped fuel the Industrial Revolution. The advent of the literate society and the keeping of written records for commerce and trade were important contributions introduced to Europe by the Romans.

Although the monasterial movement degraded much of the writings of the Greeks and the Romans and severely hampered the distribution of learning into the common everyday experience of the average citizen, in many instances the monasteries also led to local awareness of individual regions and the development of towns and villages around such a theme or central point.

As Lewis Mumford points out in *The City in History*, the development of a trilogy of power was fundamental to the manner in which the English-speaking world and western Europe developed. The rise of the merchant class as a fundamental part of the nation and society and, with its recognition, the social approval and acceptance of private enrichment through trade and commerce rather than solely through royal favoritism or blood, or religious sanction or worship—both emphasized by the strength of the military—was a fundamental change in the structure of societies leading into the Industrial Revolution era. For it was precisely such characteristics that led to the growth of local communities in population and affluence, and also led to the formation of leagues and associations between cities and communities for the protection that such group affiliation could bring; and, at the same time, such affiliations usually had some common base in trade and commerce to cement the bond between them.

It was at about this stage of development that the development of gunpowder occurred with reference to military and artillery tactics. With the new substance of gunpowder, the older types of city defense were suddenly found to be totally inadequate. The range of the new artillery was far greater than arrows, crossbows, or spears. This capacity far overcame the previous limitations of rivers, moats, or even defensive walls, such as dated back to times of ancient Jericho.

As a result of this new technology the old types of towns, with their walls and moats, were quickly found to be indefensible. The only way to adequately defend communities and towns was through the group allegiance of towns into nations that could mutually defend an invasion of one of the member towns. Also, through mutual aid and defense, the costs of bigger and much more expensive defenses could be defrayed through the group rather than having one town burdened with the entire effort.

As a consequence of this new emphasis on defensive association, and the huge expansion of defensive structures and design, the cities and towns were forced to grow internally for the first time. Life in the areas outside the city defenses was not safe or secure for much of the population; also it was more attractive to live inside the security of the citadels or defenses of the city than to be subjected to the uncertainties of life outside the city. During this period of time, the city added a new incentive to its residents. Not only were the economic advantages of city living enough to retain people as well as attract new residents, but now the security offered by the city and its administration and allegiances was another strong force in attracting new residents and keeping the older citizens.

With a growing population, most cities of the late Middle Ages found that such population was putting increasing pressure on the city itself, for the huge structure and space-consuming designs of the defensive network of the city prevented growth from occurring in an outward direction. As a result, the growth that did occur took place inside the city defenses. This growing density of citizens inside the city led to all but the elimination of open areas for agriculture, parks, and recreation.

The city of the Middle Ages progressively grew more dense in population, less green and open, and characteristically dark and dreary. The formerly artistic and handsome architecture, and open courts and fountains, yielded to the pressure of the growing populations. The buildings became less massive and decorative, and began to rise to three and four floors in an attempt to house more citizens in the same area that formerly was occupied by only one family structure.

The sanitation and public services necessary to support such rising populations started to become overburdened, and there was little significant improvement over the systems originally built by the Romans. Indeed, after throwing off Roman domination, many of even those public facilities were neglected and abused to the point where that level of service was no longer sustained.

THE BLACK PLAGUE

Beginning in southern Europe in 1347, the bubonic plague spread in a series of epidemics through 1350 and covered all Europe from the Mediterranean to Scandinavia and from Russia through Britain. Although bubonic plague had appeared even in the Greek Empire before the time of Christ, it reached its harrowing proportions in the Middle Ages from the 1300s up into the 1700s. As we know now, bubonic plague is carried by fleas borne by the rat population. The filth and unsanitary conditions which characterized the major cities at this time were largely responsible for huge rat and rodent populations that existed within such cities. The plague was largely a city-borne and city-endured phenomenon, for which the living conditions and health conditions of the time were responsible. The lack of knowledge as to the real cause of bubonic plague accounts to a large extent for why such a threat cast its shadow over Europe and most of the world for several hundred years.

ECONOMIC IMPACT OF THE PLAGUE

For much of the Middle Ages the plague caused major economic changes throughout much of Europe. The dreary life of the common city dweller in a city of primitive sanitation facilities, inadequate water supply, and very high density, was made even worse by the threat of disease. The rich and powerful could leave the city to the sanctuary of some country home or palace; the poor had to stay in the city even during the epidemics of plague. As a result there was a massive loss of life, which often ran as high as one-third or one-half of the total population of the city, and resulted in a huge drop in the demand for food-stuffs from the surrounding country farms.

The loss of a market for the foodstuffs grown by farmers led to the loss of income on the part of the farming population. This loss of income often resulted in the loss of farms. When the farmer could not find sources of income adequate to support his family, the city offered the only remaining market for the skills of a talented farmer in the areas of the crafts and trades of the time.

The second part of the deadly cycle was the increase of city population after a plague epidemic by the influx of the former farming population. The farmers also suffered from the ravages of the plague; the economic importance was the fact that in many instances those who survived fled the unprofitable farming communities and immigrated to the cities.

PHILOSOPHICAL CHANGES

A much more subtle and less evident impact of the plague epidemics was the changes in moral and philosophical fiber of the populations. The role of the Church, as the one common and uniformly accepted moral and philosophical standard of the nations of that time, was drastically altered by the experiences of the plague. The populations of cities and towns soon found that their religious leaders were not powerful enough to prevent the morally good and devout citizen from suffering the ravages of the plague.

The Reformation began during this time in human history, and many other religious movements also established a following in contradiction to the formerly all-powerful and central role of the Catholic Church. The scene of people gathered at a tavern or dance hall and behaving as though there were no tomorrow and that it didn't make much difference if there were, was a too-frequent picture in the times of the ravages of the black plague. The important thing, from the standpoint of the present study, was the change of emphasis that occurred in terms of the role of the individual in the determination of a person's individual success in a career of his or her choice.

The idea of what has been termed as the "Protestant Ethic" was born in the climate that preceded as well as included the Industrial Revolution. The idea that through hard work and commitment a person could make a success of himself was born at this time, and former ideas of idleness and nonproductive activities were discarded. The saying that "the devil makes use of idle hands," which many of us have heard as children, was illustrative of the philosophy that grew out of the moral climate after the plague and during the Industrial Revolution.

The importance of this change in moral attitude is important to the sequence of events that followed after and during the beginning of the industrialization of the world. The concept that an inventor or a clever manufacturer could benefit directly from the introduction or application of a technical idea or invention was new in terms of practical aspects of such a thought.

The role of the religious leader or monarch was not so complete or all-pervasive after the Reformation. The concept of individual self-worth was new to much of human thought. The favor of the king or prince, or the approval of the clergy or religious leaders of the community, were no longer the sole way in which inventions and adaptions could be introduced into the economic world of events. The role of the merchant was much independent of the prince and the priest. The merchant could adapt or try new ideas of inventions at will, and then reap the results—both positive and negative—himself.

THE INDUSTRIALIZATION
OF SOCIETY

The Industrial Revolution is really more appropriately called the "mechanical and energy revolution." The two major changes in the way mankind conducted personal affairs were the substitution for machine power, of manpower and the harnessing of energy sources which provided the power for much of that substitution.

The one major characteristic of the Industrial Revolution was that such a change in technology required one major thing for its existence: The switch from manpower to machine power must be more profitable in terms of cost of production than the continuance of manpower. The output from the same plant must increase substantially in order to result in a lower cost per unit; or the scale of production must increase to such a point that previous markets could not be served because of limited capacity. In either case, the one major precondition is a market large enough and affluent enough to accommodate the new output.

The second major condition of industrialization is an available labor pool large enough to fill the needs of industry that grows around such initial industrialization. Rather than reducing the labor base of a sector of the economy, the process of industrialization actually increases the need for labor to a much greater extent than that which existed prior to mechanization.

Recalling that the Industrial Revolution has been described as the "English revolution," the military problems of Europe, with the advent of artillery when compared to the natural "moat" of the English Channel, tends to explain to a great extent why the Industrial Revolution has been widely recognized as starting in the British Isles. In addition, the natural resources, such as coal and running water, and deep-water and protected ports, and a sophisticated system of canals, were all part of the collective causes and contributors to the industrialization of the British Isles.

The philosophical changes that occurred during the Middle Ages, especially during and after the epidemics of the black plague, were also changes evident in the societies and power structure of the British Isles. Also, since the Norman Conquest in 1066, the language base of the British was not totally separate from the language base in the majority of the trading world. Since trade is a vital part of industrialization, this was no small event or contributory cause of the success of the Industrial Revolution.

THE IMPORTANCE OF TRADE

As we have seen from the very beginnings of urbanization, trading has been one of the two major types of economic causes of settling. When a sector of an economy becomes mechanized, the multiplication of labor through such mechanization results in an increase of output or production. This increase in production tends to produce a surplus beyond the needs for local consumption. Shortly such a surplus finds its way into the marketplaces of other areas through trade and export. The major reasons for this acceptance of trade is the lowered price of the product of the industrialized sector, or a new or better product than that which was available before industrialization. As a result of the importance as well as the advantages associated with trade, the first nations to become industrialized also tended to be those with the largest trading base either before or shortly after industrialization.

Trading, being a reciprocal arrangement between two or more areas, also resulted in the trading areas generating more goods and products than other areas not able to take advantage of trade. The industrial nation would find a growing market for its products, and the resource-rich nation would find a growing demand for its resources. Both areas would benefit from the existence of trade that was growing and expanding.

FACTORS OF URBANIZATION

In the trends that were established after the outbreak of industrialization, the four factors of production—land, labor, capital, and technology—began to shift in their relative importance.

Traditionally land was the single most important element in the development and urbanization of mankind. The existence of fertile and highly productive agricultural land, or the land areas at crucial junctures in trade, were the most important elements in the location and size of cities.

With the advent of industrialization, labor and land suddenly changed positions, and capital and technology were added to those major determinants of urban growth. Industry by definition requires accessible and adaptable labor pools in sufficient supply. Industrialization also requires a large investment in capital and productive resources.

In Europe, and particularly in the British Isles, there existed a three-legged economy of the Church, the monarchy, and the mercantile class that contributed greatly to the process and the very possibility of industrialization. Through the former feudal estates, the land and agriculture existed—even if in a diminished state from the time before the plague epidemics. There was also the existence of a rather well-to-do merchant class, which also had capital resources available with which to take advantage of opportunities within such markets.

Finally, by this time there were also many cities in Europe and the British Isles that contained populations well into the thousands. Under such conditions, and when combined with the assumption of capitalism, it did not take long for ideas of a profit-generating nature to find their way into the world of commerce and trade as well as manufacturing. For under such assumptions as are true under capitalism, the inventor and the applicator of inventions could reap the profits of his idea to the material as well as the social benefit of his station in life. It was through this way that technology tended to develop and was applied to commerce and industry.

TRENDS OF URBANIZATION WITH INDUSTRY

Two major factors helped to determine the location and development of cities in the late 1700s and the 1800s. First, there was the harnessing of energy sources for the huge demands of industry. Natural resources, such as beds of easily obtainable coal for forging and heating, and natural waterfalls of reasonable size that enable the development of water wheels for mass production, were two of the early factors contributing to the location and size of cities.

A second major element closely intertwined with the first was the available transportation system of the area. Initially the presence of a slow navigable river or waterway was important as the source of needed raw material or energy resources. Cities such as Liverpool, London, Amsterdam, Chicago, and New York, are examples of cities with a varied degree of raw materials in a natural state within their limits or borders. All five cities have a key advantage in their location on key junctions in the transportation systems of their respective nations in the 1800s. The importance of transportation cannot be overemphasized in terms of the location development pattern of urban centers in the world prior to the 1900s.

There are, and were, a few examples of cities which grew in spite of their disadvantages in terms of transportation. Usually the reasons were either that raw material was extremely valuable and rare (such as gold and oil) or they soon overcame those initial transportation problems through compensating transportation methods, such as the Middle and Far West, with the building of the transcontinental railroad. Those areas that did not overcome their transportation problems and also began to deplete their natural resources base had nothing to fall back on and soon perished as urban centers. Examples are areas such as the gold rush cities of the Upper Yukon Valley, and the mining towns lying empty and dying throughout the western part of the United States.

Other towns which overcame transportation problems to become growing metropolitan and/or urban centers would include: San Francisco, Seattle, Denver, and many others of less notable nature. Through competitive advantage such as transportation can offer, even in those instances where the original cause of town formation has gone by, transportation advantage can often improve on the economic base of an area to the extent of totally displacing the original cause of growth and prosperity. One example is the exhaustion of the goldfields in the San Francisco area.

The Industrial Revolution introduced the concentration of skills and crafts in the large urban centers, and, in effect, led to the draining of the skilled workers from the former village and town industries of much smaller scale. In turn this led to cities becoming composed of several areas where workers with similar skills concentrated. Just as in today's city where people are concentrated in terms of economic level, in the newly industrialized towns workers tended to concentrate according to industry or trade. Mill workers, miners, textile workers, and so on, tended to live with other mill workers, miners, textile workers, and the like.

The gap between owners and workers was inclined to be a very big one. Only the wealthy owners gained sufficient stature in the community to feel secure in living outside the industry social climate to which their workers were married.

Nearly every single large city of the Industrial Era was located at a crucial junction in the transportation network. Furthermore, its location was very largely a function of natural conditions of climate, geography, and geology. Natural bays and ports, protected from severe weather conditions or the rough water of the open seas, were initially the principal points at which cities of industry developed.

THE STEEL INDUSTRY

The development and refinement of the production process of steel and iron alloys was a major step in the Industrial Revolution. Mass production of steel tools and machine parts for farming led to increased production, a very necessary precondition or simultaneous condition for industrialization. The mass production of consumer items, and other items consumed by city dwellers and exchanged in foreign trade, provided the initial momentum for the bulk of the Industrial Revolution.

The steel industry also dictated some of the major urban center formations of the 1800s. Cities such as Pittsburgh, Erie, and Chicago were located along key water transportation routes where the bulk commodities necessary for the production of steel, such as iron ore, coal, limestone, were shipped by barge to the large mills in the area. Similar towns in Europe and Britain were ushered into the Industrial Era of large urban centers because of their key locations close to natural resources necessary for steel production and the location of key water transportation routes. In fact, the presence of a viable and large steel industry became the major distinguishing feature of developed nations as opposed to those nations termed undeveloped.

This same crude classification of industrial progress continued after World War II. The case of the Philippine Islands gaining a steel mill at the time of independence from the U.S. is a prime example of the worship of steel as the key to development. The Philippines have no coal, no iron ore, and little limestone. Neither do they have a large concentration of industries dependent on steel for production. And yet they have a steel mill which they had hoped would bring their nation into the category of a developed industrialized country, based on the assumption that they were not already developed and full-fledged members of the developed world.

TRANSPORTATION

The Industrial Revolution could equally be described as a revolution in the transportation of goods and people. For the old methods of horse-drawn carriage, or mule and oxen carts, simply were not adequate to accommodate the volume and needs of the industrial sectors. Water transportation was the key mode of transport for industry at the beginnings of the Industrial Revolution, primarily barge and ocean sailing vessels. But the number of areas with a developed network of rivers, lakes, and canals was quite small in relation to the scope of the industrialized world as we know it.

Initially, locations with such unique advantages in waterways were the first to become large industrial cities. In some instances the natural resources were so attractive as to make it a profitable investment to build canals joining previously separated waterways, such as the Erie Canal. Not all products or commodities, and especially people, were well suited to the slow and tedious journeys involving river and canal barge traffic.

The advent of the railroad was the first major breakthrough in the transportation problems associated with the Industrial Revolution. Now whole new areas could be developed for their natural resources, or natural trade advantages, that previously were out of the question because of the lack of adequate waterways and/or ports to accommodate shipping and trade. Nowhere were the advantages more obvious than in the North American continent. The land mass was so large that without adequate land transportation facilities, the advantages of such rich natural resources were to lie untouched until land transportation systems could be applied.

The railroad also had another big advantage over the water transportation systems that were available at that time. The railroad was much faster than the barge or riverboat traffic of its time. As such, it provided an ability to move goods and products which previously could not be moved fast enough to maintain their quality by water-borne transportation systems. Things such as perishables, which could spoil, and fragile items such as furniture and personal items, could also be handled on the railroads due to the lower amount of handling and transfer of cargo involved in railroad traffic. The final type of items more suitable to railroad traffic, and far more efficient by rail, was the transportation of people and also animals.

RAILROADS AND URBANIZATION

Because rail transportation by its very nature is more efficient when the stops are far apart so that speed can be maintained between stopping points, train stations tended to attract development on a much larger scale than the previous land systems of stage and carriage. Because of the increased payload of trains, they also encouraged development on a much larger scale than most of the water routes in the landlocked areas.

Thus some of the major cities to become established during the past 150 years, especially in the United States, have been those cities that were able to attract and win a railhead position in their community. With such a railroad base for a community, the dependent areas affected by the railroad access soon began to congregate in those communities. With the growing economic base, the service and consumer industries soon followed. This led to great growth for many cities such as Denver, Spokane, Portland, and many others in the western and midwestern parts of the United States.

THE AUTOMOBILE ERA

The next great breakthrough in transportation was the development of the automobile industry. In less than 75 years, the automobile and trucking industries have grown to be among the largest in the world. The single case of General Motors Corporation is awesome in its growth. From not even one dollar in sales 75 years ago, that company would now rank as one of the largest and most productive nations in the world—if it were counted as a nation in terms of its total assets and sales per year.

Not only the growth of the industry itself has been phenomenal, but the huge spillover impact on other industries has been tremendous. One need only think for a moment about the petroleum industry, the auto parts and service industry, and the monstrous size of the commitment on the part of the public sector in terms of roads, highways, bridges, and traffic control and policing, to realize the impact of the automobile on the contemporary way of life in most developed or urbanized parts of the world.

The advent of the concept of suburbia and its attendant implications since the end of World War II is laid largely at the doorstep of the development and trends in the automobile industry. The reckless manner in which much of the urban development has been planned for during the past 30 years has been an outgrowth of the human being's love affair with the automobile. The pollution and congestion, with their accompanying levels of frustration on our (the participants') part in our morning and evening journey to and from work and play, have had some major impact on those areas most highly affected. The higher wages demanded to subsidize citizens who have to live in areas such as New York or Los Angeles attest to the inability of planners and their affiliated politicians to accommodate the demands and effects of the automobile.

The tremendous flexibility provided by the motoring industry has also had some dramatic impact on the way in which urban areas have grown during the past 30 years. Rather than being confined to a highly congested area with overhigh densities throughout the day, the automobile and truck allows people to live away from the highly congested and centralized working areas demanded by an industrialized society. The contemporary problem appears to be that even this ability has now been exceeded by the magnitude of growth which has occurred on the horizontal plain, and the continuing trends of people to live in urban areas or in their close suburban counterparts.

THE AIRLINE INDUSTRY

The introduction of the airplane had a dramatic impact on certain areas of conduct or concern, but it did not greatly affect the patterns of land use and urbanization in the majority of urban settlements established prior to the introduction of the airplane. Some areas—such as major cities of international trade and politics—were altered by the introduction of the airplane, as were some of the more remote areas of interest to tourists and natural resource industries. The influence of the airplane steadily grew to the point where now it is of major concern in most large urban areas.

The cause of the increased impact of the airline industry on the local residents and politicians has not been on the advantages and growth associated with this relatively new mode of transportation. Rather the huge demand on land area by airports and their affiliated industries and the ill effects on the population by air and noise pollution have been the main reasons for the increase in general concern about airlines. Unlike all other major modes of transportation, the airlines do not have to bear the burden of investing in and maintaining their terminal facilities. The airports and terminals are nearly always provided by the public sector at large, and the airlines are then charged landing fees of various types. As the people own and maintain such facilities, they have a great deal to say about where such facilities will be located and the size that such facilities will be.

MAJOR FACTORS OF URBANIZATION IN THE INDUSTRIAL ERA

As in the ancient cities already discussed in the previous chapter, the cities of the Industrial Revolution depended on the health and development of viable agricultural and trading sectors. There were, however, some major changes which helped to account for the scale of development after the Industrial Revolution had begun.

AGRICULTURE

First there was the harnessing of powerful energy sources and their application to the lives of the citizens. Through wind and water power, and later steam and coal, activities could be accomplished that would have been totally impossible or impractical using only human or animal labor. Even in those areas where the power sources were applied to existing trades or activities, the efficiency and the lowered unit cost as production expanded soon displaced those continuing to produce such items with human and animal labor. Either the existing sectors incorporated the new techniques, or they were soon reduced to ghost towns because of their inability to compete.

INDUSTRIALIZATION

The second major factor of influence was the inherent characteristic of industry itself. Because of the greater output, greater quantities of inputs were required. These inputs included the total pool of labor within the company. The labor employed was not the same skilled type of preindustrialization, but rather a new skill or semiskill. Requirements for massive amounts of inputs, as well as large markets to sell the output, gave great impetus to move the population of many countries to become more city dwellers than country dwellers. The demands of industry created the economic incentives to attract people into the major industrialized towns. The technology of that same industrial sector created the methods through which higher density and larger cities could be maintained and supported with the necessary facilities required of large urban centers.

TRANSPORTATION

The third major influence in the patterns and scale of urbanization during the Industrial Revolution was the breakthroughs in the transportation thresholds which restricted human activity until this time. The mobility provided to people and goods was tremendous. The new land transportation systems also allowed the economic development of natural and agricultural resources that were part of the necessary base inputs for further expansion. The multiplication of labor in the agricultural sector through machinery and transportation of inputs and product outputs allowed the employment of excess labor in the industrial sector. The transportation sector also drastically changed the former patterns of city development in terms of the actual land use patterns within the cities themselves. Probably no single other factor influenced the patterns of city development and the life styles of city dwellers more than the railroad and automotive industries.

CULTURAL CHANGE

Finally the structural changes which occurred within the culture of civilized man provided what I believe was a major factor in both the timing of the Industrial Revolution, and in the degree of development and acceptance of the changes associated with such industry. The adoption of the capitalistic outlines and resultant growth of the merchant class during this period in human history were crucial in terms of the rate of growth in the industrialized sectors and in the coming to power of the industrialized nations of the world.

POST-INDUSTRIALIZATION

THE RISE OF CONSUMERISM

If there is any difference between the patterns of urbanization during the Industrial Revolution and the patterns of development being witnessed in the contemporary world, it would most likely lie in the degree of consumption, or consumer products, as compared to production items or capital items as a proportion of the total output of the production sector. Partial evidence of this shift from production to consumption is the growth in sectors of the economy, such as government employment and the service industries. One need only glance at the size of Washington, D.C. in terms of total population to see the impact of the service industries on American life. Many of the industrialized nations of the world have equally as noticeable examples of the growth of the service sector, as opposed to the production sectors as evidence of a subtle but definite shift from production to consumption.

This trend toward consumer goods and services on the part of nearly every industrial country in the world is a relatively recent shift in emphasis on the part of the economies of such countries. In fact the industrialized countries themselves are quite recent in terms of the history of urbanization over the past 10,000 or 12,000 years. A mere 100 to 200 of those years have witnessed the accelerated growth and development associated with the Industrial Revolution. Such a recent development and of such short duration is the era of industrialization that it certainly is not clear whether industrialization has led to a new revolution of consumption.

Although the Babylonians, the Greeks, and the Romans eventually slid into economies that were self-destructive from an economic point of view, and although they also were very much consumer- and pageant-oriented toward their end, the shift toward affluence and social programs in contradiction to economic principles on the part of contemporary societies of the developed world is not sufficiently established to warrant an alarm.

SELECTED READINGS

Bronowski, J. *The Ascent of Man*. Boston, Mass.: Little, Brown and Company, 1973.

Comhaire, Jean, and Werner J. Chanman. *How Cities Grew*. 4th ed. Florham Park, N.J.: Florham Press, 1971.

Davis, Kingsley. *Cities: Their Origin, Growth, and Human Impact*. San Francisco, Calif.: W. H. Freeman Company, 1973.

Mumford, Lewis. *The City in History*. New York: Harcourt, Brace and World, Inc., 1961.

Smith, Adam. *An Inquiry into the Nature and Causes of the Wealth of Nations*. Chicago: Encyclopedia Britannica, Inc., 1952.

PART TWO

GROWTH

In the preceding chapters we have established the origins of the trend toward urbanization on the part of the human race and the economic forces which prevailed in history and up to the present time. We shall now discuss the causes of the various phases of urbanization. We have seen that this process of conversion of the human being from a nomadic and agricultural gatherer to the city dweller of specialized skills and numerous detailed interests has continued for more than 10,000 years. We have also seen that the history of urbanization, as a factor contributing to and resulting from the process of industrialization, is a very brief part of the total history of urbanization.

We now turn our attention to the concept of growth, and more particularly to the growth of urbanized centers. The ills of the past, although perhaps not the result of design but of ignorance, have made many people painfully aware of some ills associated with rapid urbanization. The current social and political focus on managed, slow, or no-growth policies on the part of municipal, county, state, and even the federal government, is an indication of the importance of the concept of growth from the economic perspective.

CHAPTER THREE

THE CONCEPT OF GROWTH

MORE OF EVERYTHING

The simplest definition of more of everything in the physical sense is not as absurd or uncommon as it first appears. (More people, more buildings, more land, more public services, more roads, more industry, are all surely indicative of a growth process.) The major problem of defining such growth is: What if everything is not expanding, or everything is not expanding at the same rate, then do we still have growth? What if only a few sectors are expanding, or only one, do we then still have growth?

Another major problem with such a simple definition of growth is the problem of measuring growth in terms usable for making decisions in the public as well as private sectors. (When every sector is included in the definition of growth, it becomes impossible to measure the rate or extent of growth in any useful way. More people is not necessarily growth in a real sense, especially if those additional people are very poor in both monetary and skill terms. If, however, those additional people were manufacturers, and the employees were working at new facilities, then such additions to the population would indeed be a positive sign of economic growth.

Likewise the annexation of surrounding land areas by a town or city does not indicate growth in the economic sense. Such annexation may be with the intent of controlling or preventing growth in a community before it occurs. Expansion of the public sector prior to actual growth is also very common in the area of road building and other public services. The major attraction is the much lower land acquisition costs in predeveloped areas, as opposed to the high cost of acquiring right-of-way in already established urban areas.

NATIONAL VS. STATE AND LOCAL PERSPECTIVE

It is a very small consolation to the unemployed worker that more people are employed in more sectors of the nation than ever before, or that the rate of unemployment is the lowest in recorded history. He is still without a job. It is also of little importance to the town depending on a rubber plantation that aerospace is the fastest growing industry, or that electronics shows the greatest growth potential of all industry categories. Such information would be of little relevance on a rubber plantation that is not suitable for anything else, and which has been displaced by a cheaper and yet as suitable substance produced synthetically.

Additionally the increased mobility of the populations of the more developed nations makes it very misleading to cite national trends as the major reasons for local decisions. The trends in migration, marriage, divorce, death rate, and birth rate may vary in the extreme from one area or region to another. As a result, the demand for housing, products, services labor, and many other items would also greatly vary. Real property, more than nearly any other item, tends to reflect these locational differences more than other factors. Since real property constitutes more than half of the total assets of the United States, and most probably nearly that or more in other developed countries, the causes of growth and the definition of the concept of growth from an economic perspective must be addressed. Therefore the differences between a national, regional, or state trend in growth and the growth experience of an individual community are very important.

Even within a municipality there are significant differences in the growth patterns of individual industries, firms, and neighborhoods, which must be taken into account for the decision-making forces to be productive. An analysis should include a complete and thorough study of the assets and the liabilities of a region, city, or area, in an attempt to accurately identify those areas suitable for growth as measured against both economic and social costs which the community will bear in the event of such growth.

GROWTH DEFINED AS A SINGLE FACTOR

The exact opposite of the definition of growth as more of everything, is the definition of growth as the increase in only a specific category. Growth in the number of people in an area is sufficient to conclude that there is in fact a growth in the economy of a region or locality. Likewise the growth in capital in local area banks is not evidence of absolute growth in the economy of an area. Sudden increases in the deposits in a local banking industry may be seasonal; they may also represent a shift of assets from less secure investments to the insured savings and checking accounts.

Increases related to the monetary system are often used, such as dollar volume of sales, payrolls, assessed valuation, and many others. The important point in observing numbers stated in dollar terms is the pervasive influence of inflation on such figures. If the rate of inflation locally as well as nationally has been 8 percent, and the dollar volume of sales went up a mere 5 percent, then one may make a strong case for a real 3 percent decline in that particular sector. Similarly if the dollar volume in sales was 11 percent, then one may stand a chance of being more correct in concluding that the specific industry involved was indeed growing.

One industry, however, does not a city or region make—unless that industry is very basic in the economy of such a city or region. Probably the single area where monetary policy and money systems are affected most is in the area of international trade. Where one country lowers the value of its currency relative to that of a trading partner, that country's balance of trade in terms of its own currency will rise significantly. A rise may reflect increased trade through lower prices as a result of the devaluation process, but the major increase in dollar volume, or whatever currency they have, will be the result of a change in the unit of measure rather than any real growth in the activities of the nation's or region's economy.

INCREASE IN POPULATION

A growth in the population of an area may or may not reflect a growth in the economy of that area. If the growth is by way of births, these new members of the community represent a burden of support on the part of the current mature population of that area. The new members are not a viable economic force in the community in terms of the growth of the economy.

If the growth of the population is a result of refugees or other displaced persons without funds, and very often without means of livelihood or communication, these new members of the region are significant contributors to the overall economic well being of the community. In both cases the new infants and children and the refugees represent very real drains in terms of the social and supportive services supplied on the part of the public sector, for which the community can expect no sudden increase in the level of economic activity as a result of such expenditures. Public services, such as schools, hospitals, public housing, welfare support programs, and many other socially desirable facilities, constitute an increased burden on the local economy. As funds and productivity are taken from the productive sector and placed into the public sector, the overall level of economic health in the region is lowered.

Where the increase in population is a result of the increase in the productive areas of a community, then a rise in population may be regarded as a somewhat more reliable indicator of growth. An increase in the productive sector of the economy may be in manufacturing, such as the auto and steel industries experienced in the middle and late 1800s and early 1900s; or it may reflect an increase in the productivity of the service sector, such as the financial districts and money centers of several of the major cities of the world. The growth of these industries was greater than the growth in the labor pools currently existing in such centers. As a result, the benefits increased to the point of attracting larger labor pools of certain characteristics demanded by growing industries.

GROWTH IN ASSESSED VALUATION

The value of land and structures within an area is the major source of revenue through property taxes. Growth in this item is therefore of major concern on the part of local politicians and administrators and indirectly of interest to the individual property owners of an area. When a new factory is constructed within a taxing district, the value added to the tax base is a new addition to the revenue available for public expenditures. This growth may lead to supportive policies on the part of a region which tend to attract more industry and growth. However, it may also lead to a reduction in the public debt of a region which does not act as a major contributor in terms of attracting new industry.

An increase in valuation may or may not have any correlation to the level of economic activity of a region. Where such increase in value is the result of new net additions to the employment base of an area, then the impact of growth is wide and significant. But where new additions are merely replacements of older facilities of equal size, or where new facilities are completely automated and result in very little increase in human involvement, then in such cases the rise in assessed valuation is nothing more than an increase in money for the local budget and is not growth in the real sense of the term.

TOWARD A RATIONAL
DEFINITION OF GROWTH

When we focus our attention on the concept of growth, what we really have in mind is the growth in the use and productivity of the sector of the region known as the real property sector. Until there are noticeable changes in the manner and intensity of the use of land resources, most growth is too obscure to require much attention. Therefore growth may well be defined as a change in the pattern of use of land from a less intensive use toward a more intensive use of land resources. The increase in the intensity of the use of land by definition increases the productivity of the land area in question.

Examples of such land use intensity changes would be the shift from agricultural land use to the development of single family homes on the same land. More people would be occupying the same amount of land area than before; there would also be a dramatic rise in the amount of capital and material resources committed to the same land area as before.

The replacement of older single-family buildings with more compact and better planned condominiums and hotels, with perhaps some retail and commercial use, would likewise increase the productivity of the same land area as before. Although the first case would most probably entail the growing of a city outward in geographical and physical terms, the second example would not involve the physical expansion of the city, and at the same time surely should be considered real growth. The focusing of our attention on the use and intensity of land use within the urban areas in our attempts to define growth comes much closer to a workable and very real and practical definition of the term growth.

Thus growth, in the economic sense, may be better defined as an increase in the intensity of use to which the land resources are put. This may be a function of more people using the same land area as before, or it may include factors other than people— such as higher capital investment in the same land area; more material investment; or increased productivity associated with a given land area as measured in terms of real dollar sales; or transfers of products or services of that particular land area.

An example of the last type would be the changing of land use to a more profitable and growth-oriented product line than the product or service previously coming from the land area concerned. It is also important to note that such a definition of growth as we have developed would not require the segregation of industries because they were basic or nonbasic industries, or because they were basic or nonbasic industries in that area, but merely whether they were more productive now than some time in the recent past, or more productive than the industry type previously occupying the land.

Such a definition also avoids the problem of defining the various stages of growth that have been employed in the many analyses of growth in the past. The problems of establishing the exact parameters of each stage in the growth process, and clearly identifying the transition from one stage to another within a time frame that is meaningful, are both avoided in using a concept of growth based on the use of land resources and the changes in patterns of use which are already established.

TIME FRAME OF THE ANALYSIS

In an attempt to analyze the growth process, one must be very careful to establish the time frame of the study. It is clearly apparent that land use changes on a parcel-by-parcel survey are more meaningful to the immediate or short-range type of analysis. If one is interested in general policy development on a country, city, state, or regional basis, then the time frame of concern is much longer than the changes on a small parcel-by-parcel basis. The well established trends in terms of overall land use patterns and changes, as well as the overall health of the various industry segments, are of more concern to the general policy analyst.

For the individual owner or investor, however, the changes in land use patterns and intensity within and surrounding his or her property interest is of much greater concern. Insofar as one is interested in the smaller scale or view of a neighborhood, or surrounding property owners of a subject property, then the time frame of concern is not in the long-term trends but rather in the month-to-month or year-to-year trends which may be short-lived but are still very important to individual properties and their owners.

The time-lag in such information as may affect adjacent properties is much shorter than the statistics which are far outdated by the time they reflect the trends of an entire region or community. For that reason the reliance that may be on the short-run statistics reflecting contemporary events and trends is, or tends to be, much more well founded than the state often accorded the massive figures and presentations of the more thorough and more outdated studies of the planning community of professionals.

SCALE OF THE ANALYSIS

Just as the time frame of the analysis is an important qualification of the reliability of the approach employed, so also is the scale of the subject which the observer is studying. If one is interested in the near future trends that will affect the value and therefore the use of the small residential lot, what the student would attempt to gather in terms of data would be far less extensive than if the perspective involved the entire land use future of the city, state, or nation.

One of the major problems in the study of urban land use patterns is the problem of meaningful studies with reliable data that are not out of date. The larger the scope of the examination, the more time-consuming the data collection phase of research becomes. As a result of the extended time involved in collecting data, the basic informational inputs of the study are quickly outdated. The way in which most studies overcome a problem of this kind is to make the study very broad and theoretical so that the exact details of the analysis are less meaningful than the general trends on a regional, state, or national basis.

With reference to the land use definition of growth, a broad study would perhaps look at the total acreage subject to changes in land use. Then by comparing such trends with established levels of use in the larger cities or areas, the researcher may support the conclusion that the subject area was growing in the direction of the larger cities already established. The private investor or student, however, would look at the detailed changes in land usage surrounding his area of interest. The changes in neighborhood composition and physical state of the land use of the area would be immediate data of current trends that would affect the subject area in the current time frame and not at some time in the future.

Although such minute statistics would not be suitable for a policy decision on local, state, or national level they would provide sufficient information on which to base an immediate decision to buy, sell, improve, repair, or do nothing. After sufficient numbers of individuals make similar decisions, the total becomes large enough to draw the attention of the general planning agencies and the commitment of local administrators and politicians.

The larger policy areas are quite far removed from the immediate land use analysis and decisions, and, to a very large extent, make decisions based on the data gathered after the fact. It is for this reason that the student must establish beforehand which scale of observation is most appropriate to his study; for the entire effort will be shaped and influenced by that scale of reference, and the parameters of the data inputs involved.

SELECTED READINGS

Banfield, Edward C. *The Unheavenly City*. Boston: Little, Brown and Company, 1970.

Clawson, Marion. *Suburban Land Conversion in the United States*. Baltimore: The John Hopkins Press for the Future, 1971.

Editorial Research Reports. *The Future of the City*. Washington, D.C.: Congressional Quarterly Inc., 1974.

Editorial Research Reports. *Urban Environment*. Washington, D.C.: Congressional Quarterly Inc., 1969.

Goldsmith, Edward. *Blueprint for Survival*. Boston: Houghton Mifflin, 1972.

Meadows, Donella H., et al. *The Limits to Growth.* New York:
    Universe Books, 1972.
Whyte, William H. *The Last Landscape.* Garden City, N.Y.:
    Doubleday Co., 1968.

CHAPTER FOUR

THE DYNAMICS OF ECONOMIC GROWTH

ECONOMIC PRINCIPLES OF ALLOCATION

We have studied the process by which mankind became an urban dweller. Agricultural advantage and the intersection or interfacing of trade routes were the primary causes of urban growth beginning and continuing in areas with those advantages. The common denominator of such factors is the inherent economic gains associated with these developments.

From the early settlements of the Fertile Crescent through the Mediterranean on and into the heart of Europe, the overriding force was the benefits in terms of tangible need satisfaction that came with stable populations grouped in a manner so as to take advantage of the division of labor and the specialization of skills that such division allows. Although the primary advantage was in the agricultural sector—and indeed appears to continue to be a very real and critical one to this day—the advent of the Industrial Revolution added more possibilities to the list of factors encouraging urbanization.

Relationships established through basically economic functions tend to operate within a generalized set of relationships. The study of these relationships and processes, by which goods and services are allocated in the manner as they are, is the field of economics. Economics is defined as the study of exactly such processes and functions.

SUPPLY AND DEMAND ANALYSIS

The allocation process is seen in its greatest simplicity as the process by which one seller and a buyer enter into negotiations regarding some goods or a service, and the eventual price or value exchange that results when the seller transfers his goods or service to the buyer, and the buyer gives his money (or whatever) to the seller as his part of the exchange. Because each is behaving in a way to maximize his total benefit, and only the two are involved, it is considered a free transaction; each party being competitively equal. This scene is described as a perfect competition. Neither party has a monopoly on the product offered for exchange, and neither party can therefore unilaterally determine the price. The price as well as the quantity are determined by the market process of debate between the two individuals.

THE SUPPLY SCHEDULE

The seller of a commodity and all the sellers in one market of that commodity are called the supply schedule. Whatever price may be bid for the subject item, the suppliers in that industry are the sole source. The suppliers, however, will alter their production schedule of the goods or services to suit the returns they can expect in the market. If an item is sold at a high price, the producers or suppliers will tend to offer more for sale than if the price is low.

The assumption is that an economical man will always prefer more rather than less for the product or service he is offering for sale in the marketplace. At the very beginnings of urbanization this assumption would perhaps tend to be more true than in later years when other factors, such as morals, religion, and social consciousness, may impede purely economical self-interest.

If we looked at the supply schedule of one hypothetical supplier, it would appear much as in the following example.

PRICE	QUANTITY OFFERED
1.00	2
1.75	4
2.25	6

The price may be terms of the sellers expectations, based on a formal currency system and much past experience; or, it may reflect units of other goods or service offered in exchange for the product of the seller in the example. Nevertheless, the seller will tend to offer more for sale at a higher price than at a lower price. If we presented these three observations on a graph, they would appear much like the example in Figure 4-1.

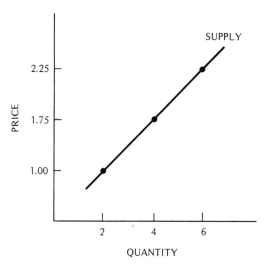

Figure 4-1 *Supply Curve*

What we now begin to see much more clearly is the slope of the supply curve upward and to the right. This slope also gives us an idea of how suppliers react to a potential rise in the price of their product, as well as to a potential drop in the market worth of their product. The positive slope of the supply schedule represents the assumption of the market analysis that the seller of a product or service will generally prefer more rather than less for his product; and where the returns are greater, there will tend to be more suppliers who are willing to produce and sell that product or service.

THE DEMAND SCHEDULE

Each buyer of a product or service individually and all the potential and actual buyers collectively constitute what is called the demand schedule. The schedule is constructed by starting with the price of a product offered for sale and the consequent level of product or service demanded by the buyers at that price. Generally as the price increases, the amount demanded by buyers in the marketplace will decline. We have the example of Ford automobiles versus Rolls-Royce automobiles. More Fords are produced and sold than Rolls-Royces. The following is a hypothetical demand schedule for the product previously described in the discussion on supply:

PRICE	QUANTITY DEMANDED
1.00	6
1.75	4
2.25	2

Just the opposite of the earlier discussed supply schedule, in the demand schedule the buyer may demand more of a product or services at a lower price than at a higher price. If we present the demand schedule on a graph, as we did with the earlier supply schedule, it would appear much as in the example in Figure 4-2. The slope of the demand schedule is exactly opposite from that of the previous supply schedule. In the demand schedule the slope is downward and toward the right, or negatively sloped. Such a line again presents more information than the mere schedule listed above. We can now see the relative degree of reaction on the part of the buyers of this product or service to a change in the price of that commodity or service.

As a potential seller of the commodity, one would be very much interested in the degree of reaction on the part of buyers

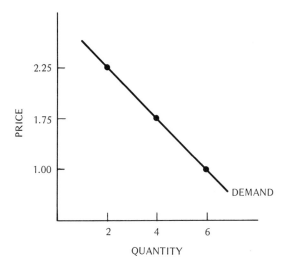

Figure 4-2 *Demand Curve*

to the lowering or raising of the price. For if one could not expect a large drop in the level of sales with a significant price rise, then the seller would be a bit naive not to raise the price and therefore his profit or returns.

As in the supply schedule presented earlier, the demand curve also represents the fundamental assumption of the market itself. The assumption that all or most buyers will generally tend to prefer to pay less rather than more for a given product or service is represented by the negative slope of the demand curve. More people will be willing to buy the subject product or service at a lower price than to buy the same product or service at a higher price.

THE MARKET CONCEPT

Where the buyer and the seller of a given product or service come to bargain and exchange is in the marketplace. When the buyers and the sellers of a given product are present, we then have a market for the specific item. Where the buyers and the sellers are present, we then can present the appropriate supply and demand curves in one graph as a valid depiction of the market. Figure 4-3 is a graph in which both the supply schedule (Figure 4-1) and the demand schedule (Figure 4-2) are presented in one graph depicting the market for a product or service. Where the desires of the sellers and the desires of the buyers are equal, then that is where the exchange of product or service will occur.

In the example, at 1.75 units of money there will be four units of product exchanged by the buyers and sellers in the market. Those sellers demanding 2.25 units for their product will not sell; and those buyers willing to pay only 1.00 units for the subject product will not be able to buy. The reason the seller will not be able to sell at 2.25 is that all buyers in the market can satisfy their needs at a price of 1.75. Likewise, the reason the buyers willing to buy only at 1.00 will not be able to buy is because all the sellers in the market can sell their product for 1.75.

Each buyer and each seller acting in his or her own self-interest will be able to enter and leave the market at will; therefore they are always tending to act in their own individual self-interest. The point at which the supply schedule intersects the demand schedule as in Figure 4-3, that is, at a price of 1.75, and at a quantity of 4 units, that point is called the market equilibrium. That is where the number of willing buyers and the number of willing sellers are equal to each other, and therefore everyone who is actively involved in the market at that time is satisfied.

It may be a temporary equilibrium, or it may be a long-run equilibrium; the market and we do not know from the market information we have available. All that we do know is that the market is operating at a point where the number of units offered for sale are all sold to a number of total units equal to the number of units buyers demand at the equilibrium price.

This hypothetical market situation is called the purely competitive model, where the degree of competition and equality between sellers and buyers is absolutely equal. Like the pure water we don't find in nature, and which would probably make us ill over time, pure competition is not found in nature or in the human experience; and if it were, we would probably find the lack of advertising and such other market imperfections annoying for the time and effort a state of such perfect competi-

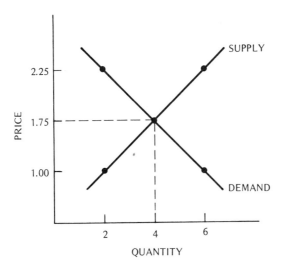

Figure 4-3   *Diagram of Market Supply and Demand Analysis*

tion would demand of the participant. Just as the use of pure water is very necessary in medical and laboratory uses and research, the concept of perfect competition is very important to the clarification of the underlying relationships and principles that govern the actions of the buyers and sellers in all markets everywhere.

THE ASSUMPTION OF PERFECT COMPETITION

Many buyers and sellers.   Sufficient number of both buyers and sellers so that no one buyer and no one seller will exert an influence over the rest of the market.

Perfect knowledge.   Perfect knowledge on the part of both buyers and sellers so that all buyers know what all other sellers and buyers are doing. It is also assumed that buyers know all there is to know about the product that all sellers are attempting to sell.

Homogeneous commodity.   The product in the market of

pure competition is a uniform standard product which is the same no matter who manufactures or sells it. The product of any one seller is identical to that of any other seller.

Free entry and exit. All buyers and all sellers are free to enter and leave the market at any time at will. It is also assumed that there is no noticeable time-lag in entering or leaving.

Free price mechanism. The sellers of a product in a purely competitive market are free to raise or lower their price in response to the market forces of the moment.

Although the above assumptions are grossly detached from the characteristics of markets found in the real world, the relationships that such simplistic examples and analyses bring out are very real indeed. For example, we do find that as the number of potential customers increases greatly relative to the supply of a product or service, it is not long until that supply is also expanded to accommodate that rise in demand.

With reference to Figure 4-3, there is first a shift of the demand schedule to the right, and then a shift in the supply schedule also to the right. Prior to the adjustment of the supply to the new demand, there is a sudden rise in the price of the item or service under examination. In the real world experience, however, there seldom is one exact and uniform price for any one product or service to all customers or buyers of that service or product. Also, because there is a department from virtually each one of the five assumptions of the perfectly competitive model, the entire market is a bit more obscure or general than the models suggest. What is probably more accurate in describing the real world market would be the situation depicted in Figure 4-4.

What we tend to find is a range of possible prices and quantities at what appears to be a market equilibrium point. Some buyers have more knowledge of the product or service, and the market of that product or service, than do other less informed buyers. As a result of such knowledge, these buyers will perhaps buy at a lower price than the less informed buyers. Likewise, some sellers are more astute than other sellers and able to merchandize and display their product more attractively than others.

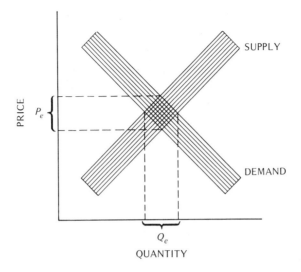

Figure 4-4 *Banded Supply and Demand Analysis*

Things other than price which tickle a buyer's fancy will have some impact on the quantity sold in the marketplace. Other things would be generally described as deviations from the purely competitive model, but nevertheless they are real and do occur in the marketplace. Thus there tends to be a range of possible prices and a range of possible quantities exchanged all at what could be described as the market equilibrium point. In Figure 4-4, such an equilibrium point would be described as the quantity Q_e at the price P_e.

THE CONCEPT OF ELASTICITY

A real key concept to the meaningful interpretation and use of the economic principles such as have been previously discussed is how much supplies and demand schedules react to changes in price or quantity changes in the marketplace. The concept of elasticity measures exactly that degree of change. When the price of a commodity rises, say, one unit, and the quantity demanded drops more than one unit, then the demand for that commodity or service is said to be relatively elastic.

Referring to Figure 4-5, if the price of a commodity rises

from P_1 to P_2 the resultant quantity demanded will drop from Q_1 back to Q_2. The decline in the amount demanded is far greater than the amount or proportional rise in price. The demand schedule in such an industry would be described as highly elastic. This would also aid those in the market in their attempts to predict what the possible reaction would be to adjustments or changes in price of the commodity under examination. The

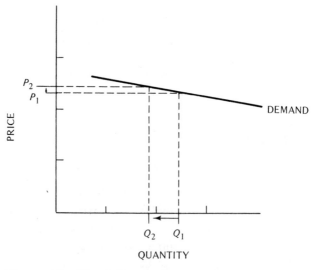

Figure 4-5 *Elastic Demand*

opposite case of a relative inelastic demand curve would be similar to that shown in Figure 4-6. With the price rising from P_1 to P_2 the resultant decline in the amount demanded is much less than the proportionate rise in price. Such a demand schedule would be described as relatively elastic. From the seller's point of view, price would be a very important factor in sales level for the product in Figure 4-5, but the price would not be a very decisive factor in the case of commodity in Figure 4-6.

The elasticity of supply is also a very important element in the marketplace, and Figures 4-7 and 4-8 depict the relatively elastic and inelastic supply schedules respectively. The elastic supply schedule reflects the fact that a small rise in price will tend to generate a relatively large increase in the amount supplied, where an inelastic supply schedule shows only a minor increase in the supply when the price increases.

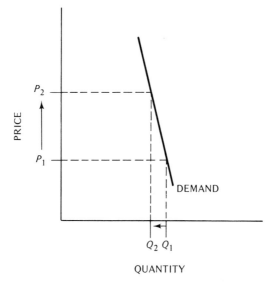

Figure 4-6   *Inelastic Demand*

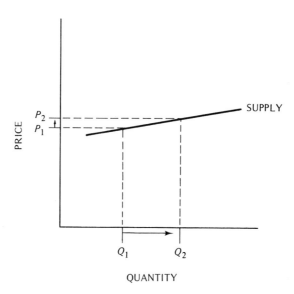

Figure 4-7   *Elastic Supply*

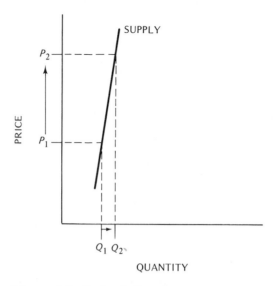

Figure 4-8 *Inelastic Supply*

REAL ESTATE AS AN
ECONOMIC COMMODITY

How does the urban community relate to the hypothetical economic models presented? What are the supply and demand characteristics of the urban real estate sector? For such over-simplified models to have much meaning or significance they must be able to be translated into the real world environment. The beginning point would seem to be to define the urban real estate sector in terms of an economic good. Real estate is not the mere physical description of so many square feet of soil in some specific geographical location. Real property is much more than that. Essentially real estate is an abstract commodity. What a person owns when owning real property is really a bundle of rights to use the real property at specific locations.

The owner of real property cannot create more land, or move his real property to accommodate the market he or she is trying to serve. If my market moves a few hundred yards away, I am unable to move my real property over to meet their needs. What the owner of real property has is really a bundle of specific rights defined by society and enforced or defined by that same society. Real estate is a usable resource, but not a consumable resource. Even in the cases of basic raw materials in the form of natural resources, in most cases the amount of material extracted is only a small part of the total actual land under the owner's title. Therefore it is apparent that real estate is different from most other goods or services exchanged in the marketplace.

FACTORS MAKING REAL ESTATE UNIQUE

Aside from having an abstract commodity, the four factors which tend to explain the uniqueness of real estate are: 1) fixed location; 2) long life; 3) large economic units; and 4) long-term decisions. The first factor of real estate, having a very fixed location, tends to explain the large variation in the price at which real estate may be exchanged for in the marketplace. Land located in the northern Arctic or in the southern Antarctic regions has very little value, if any; whereas land located on Manhattan Island in New York, or in the middle of the commercial district of Hong Kong, would have a very high value.

Even if we assumed that the physical composition of the lands involved were identically the same, the wide price differential would still remain. Virtually all the value in real estate is a result of its location. As a result of such importance placed on the location of real estate resources, the fact that such location is fixed for virtually all time becomes very crucial in the analysis of value that takes place on the part of both buyers and sellers.

The long life of real estate resources compounds the importance of the other factors associated with real estate. The truth that if a mistake is made with references to the improvement of real property through cultivation of development, and the owners of such property will have to live with the mistake for a very long time, is a truth that some learn at a very high cost. The result is that a high premium is paid on being very accurate and precise in the analysis which takes place prior to commitment to purchase or to improve or change the use of real property. Additionally the analysis that takes place in regard to the use and ownership of real property is generally placed in a time frame of several years, rather than any temporary and short-lived market condition.

The decision to improve property with a specific type of improvement involves facilities of such a long life that other potential uses for the same property are ruled out for a very long time. As a result, improvements in real property tend to remain for a long period of time whether or not they are totally justified to remain for that period of time. In those instances where a structure is misplaced, or is not suited to the area surrounding it, even there improvements tend to remain for a longer period than the community and the owner find the property totally economically useful. It does seem economical in a common sense way to destroy an unneeded five-year-old building that would normally last another 35 or more years. Except in areas of real estate where the profit motive is very refined, and where the level of analysis is quite sophisticated, improvements once made tend to remain a very long time past their economic reasons to be built.

The fact that one cannot buy a portion of real estate for the sum of one day's or one week's wages tends to alter the manner in which real estate supply and demand schedules perform in real life. The idea that one seller and one buyer enter into negotiations in the marketplace and come to a complete agreement and exchange goods and services for money or other goods and services is simply not at all true for the real estate segment of the economy. Because the prices are so high relative to most other goods in the marketplace, the incurrence of debt is now virtually a truism for the exchange of real property.

The moment one is forced to seek outside funds from third parties to finance an economic decision to purchase a product or service in the marketplace, there then becomes a decision-making process by committee rather than by one individual. Most often the lender of funds will want to appraise the transaction to determine whether the price paid was fair and equitable and that the product involved is what the seller says it is. When such is the case, we then have a loan officer, an appraiser, and a loan approval committee, and all must agree with the decision that the principal has made in the first instance. The involvement in so many additional tasks and functions also involves an extension of time in the decision-making process.

Finally real estate by its nature involves long-term decisions. Such decisions are made on the basis of firmly established trends and conditions, rather than temporary changes in the market conditions. Seasonal or annual fluctuations in real estate activity, or in the supply or demand for real estate services, are of minor significance—unless they represent significant departure from such fluctuations in the past. The extended planning and decision-making phases involving the decision to build or improve most classes of real property tend to marry the individuals involved to their ultimate decision. Therefore changes from the initial decision are often rather slow and painful for those involved.

The additional fact that the decision-making process in real estate involves so many persons, all of whom must reach or agree on the same decision, also tends to make adjustments and future changes more sluggish in coming about. The fact that a person buying a $25,000-house must go through a process of a multitude of persons, and sign a pile of documents for title transfer, where the same person could buy a $2 million-vessel with one piece of paper in one or two days, illustrates the unique characteristics of real property and the effect those unique characteristics have on the market performance of that industry.

THE SUPPLY OF REAL ESTATE SERVICES

The supply of real estate services is a bit different from the supply schedule of most commodities exchanged in the marketplace. In the first instance, the supply schedule of real estate must be broken into two major segments: The short-term supply schedule, and the long-term supply schedule. The difference is due to the fact that real estate cannot be significantly expanded in terms of improvements and services in the very short time period normally considered as the short-term. Therefore the supply of real estate in the short-term would appear much as illustrated below.

In Figure 4-9 we can see that when the demand increases, for whatever reason, the added pressure on the existing supply of real estate services brings only a very minor increase in the supply of such services in a time frame such as we have assumed in the short-term. While the supply of real estate services expanded from Q_1 to Q_2, at the same time price jumped enormously from P_1 to P_2. Although the supply of real estate services appears to be relatively fixed in the physical sense in the short-term, the slight expansion in the supply illustrated occurs when spare rooms not normally available become part of the supply schedule due to the high rents such real estate services are commanding. There is also the phenomenon of families doubling up and occupying real estate designed for and normally occupied by one family, now being occupied by two or more families.

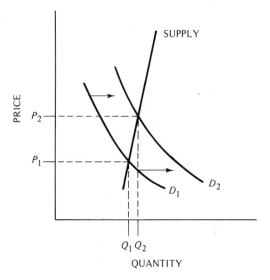

Figure 4-9 *Market Adjustment Process*

Conditions such as sudden expansions of populations because of the discovery of gold, or oil, or the building of large construction projects, such as dams or pipelines, tend to illustrate those conditions in the real world of experience. The additions to the housing stock that do occur are most often very marginal, for the time frame is again contrary to the nature of the real estate commodity. In such instances, the population increases are of a short-lived nature; whereas the nature of real estate services is that of the long run. This results in a tendency for those people who do account for the buildup in the population to be burdened with these living conditions for the complete duration of their stay in such a location, and the addition of stock to the housing supply at such a price that the owner may recover his investment in a much shorter time than the normal expected life of the real estate object itself.

Supply in the long-term behaves much differently than in the short-term. Referring again to Figure 4-9, when the price of real estate services reaches the level of P_2 in a more normal market, the investment returns associated with real property and its improvements are above those found in other types of investments of similar risk and character. When such a difference does occur, the investors in other mediums tend to withdraw their funds, and shift those monies into the real estate development and ownership areas.

When a shift of this kind occurs, it most often involves more than one person. When several individuals and development firms reach this conclusion about the prospects for real estate, they are inclined to enter that particular market in a group. This results in rather sudden expansion of the supply of real estate services in that particular market. What most often occurs is expansion beyond the point that the local market can absorb in the immediate future. As the number of unsold units climbs, and the vacancy rates climb in investment properties, there is a retreat by the same investors and land developers from the optimistic predictions of the preceding period. Generally this results in a halt in new development until the market has had sufficient time to absorb the excess supply.

The important difference between the long-term and the short-term perspective, with reference to the supply of real estate services, is that in the long-term perspective the supply of real estate services is apt to be much more elastic than during the short term. Unlike agriculture or some other markets, the real estate supply sector may be reactive to the conditions which exist in the demand sector. As a result, it takes the shifting of movement of the demand side of the ledger to cause any form of change of significance in the supply schedule. As a result of the characteristics of real estate cited earlier, the time-lags of that industry are such that there is nearly always a built-up demand prior to any real change in the supply sector.

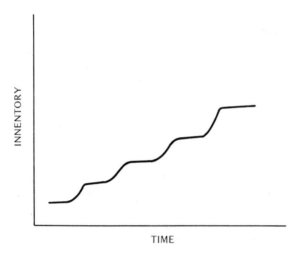

Figure 4-10 *Step Ladder Effect*

Usually such pent-up demand forces are the primary cause of the overadjustment on the part of the supply sector. Also because of the long decision-making process, and the group form of commitment that takes place in the real estate sector, once decisions are arrived at and the development monies invested, there is little likelihood that those involved will adjust their position because the market may take one year longer to absorb the complete expansion that has occurred in the supply adjustment process.

This brings up the final point to be made about the supply of real estate services. Beause of the nature of the production process in the development sector, there are generally large sums of money invested in any project before actual construction ever begins. Even after the moving of soil occurs, additional sums of sizable proportions are invested in areas other than salable products. Costs such as engineering, surveying, soil analysis, environmental impact studies, market analysis, loan commitment fees, architectural prints, and a multitude of other costs are called "sunken costs," and can often represent a significant percentage of the total cost of a project. These costs are not in any way recoverable once they have been allocated and spent, unless the total project is completed and sold.

Once such costs have been realized, and in spite of the fact that the construction of units may have been delayed for any number of reasons beyond the point of maintaining a competitive advantage in the marketplace, the developer must continue to build out the project to have any prospect at all of recovering his high sunken costs. This also tends to add to the stepladder behavior on the part of the supply schedule for real estate services in the time frame of the long term. The time frame may be several years depending on the size and type of real estate services, but most certainly it would be beyond one or two years.

THE DEMAND FOR REAL ESTATE SERVICES

Generally when we speak of the demand for real estate services, we are referring to the owner-occupant in the residential market. It may also be rather well founded to say that the demand for real estate services is likely to be more elastic than supply; therefore supply would be relatively slow to adjust to changes in the marketplace, while the demand schedule would be relatively quicker to adjust to price changes. Being, or tending to be quicker in the adjustment to changes in prices of real estate services is what we mean by the term more elastic.

Referring to Figure 4-11, it can be seen that the rise in price from P_1 to P_2 could result in a greater change in the quantity demanded, which would drop from Q_1 back to Q_2. To the extent that Figure 4-11 tends to represent the actual market in the real estate sector, one would conclude that demand is very responsive to price changes, where exactly the opposite could be true for the supply sector. It must be emphasized again, however, that what is represented in Figure 4-11 is the short-term supply and demand schedule. The long-term supply schedule might be the stepladder types previously described.

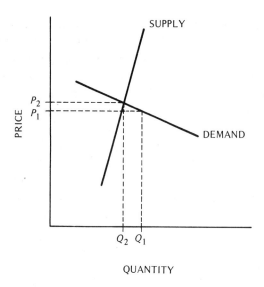

Figure 4-11 *Supply and Demand Analysis*

Although the market may generally be described as elastic, as shown in Figure 4-11, it is my opinion that Figure 4-12 might be much more accurate in describing the demand schedule for residential as well as other types of real estate services. What Figure 4-12 shows is that at the higher prices the demand for real estate services can be very inelastic. The steep slope of the demand curve shows there is little change in the quantity demanded at the higher-priced market levels. The rationale is that in the higher-priced luxury markets, the person investing in real property is committing a smaller portion of his or her total resources to that commodity than persons in the middle- and lower-priced ranges.

It is also true that there are fewer wealthy persons, so therefore the quantity could not be expected to change a great deal to fluctuations in price because of the pure numbers themselves. When prices of real property services begin too far within the range of the much larger middle class, the demand in that area becomes much greater in total and much more elastic and price sensitive. The demand function then begins to extend horizontally and thus reflect more price elasticity.

As the prices of real estate services continue to fall, the point may be reached where the demand for real estate services on the part of the great mass of the population in any area has been satisfied. A continued fall in the prices of real estate services will progressively absorb more of the very low-income levels of the citizenry. Since there tend to be as few very poor as very rich, the demand in terms of quantity desired is likely to be very less reactive to the lower prices.

Figure 4-12   *Demand for Real Estate*

As a result of this type of demand function, it can perhaps be seen why the concern of the government as well as of the majority of the citizens falls in the areas of prices for housing that fall at the very edges of the middle range. When the middle-income population finds the market reaching point (A) there may be many sectors concerned about the state of the housing market. While at the other extreme point (B) there may not be such a degree of concern on the part of the mass of the population.

At point (A), say 80 percent of the population is prevented from buying new housing because of the price. Whereas, at point (B) the same 80 percent of the population is well housed and can afford new housing. In fact, because of the rising development costs, most new housing in the United States in the middle 1970s has been very close to point (A); and because that market is so small, in terms of the number of persons able to absorb the quantity supplied, that is also the area which has seen the largest number of unsold units and developers and banks in financial troubles.

ELASTICITY OF DEMAND

There has been a great deal of study and theorizing with regard to the degree of elasticity of the demand for real estate in general, and the demand for housing in particular. Although the concept of elasticity will greatly vary depending on what the price is being compared against, it is generally true that, with reference to the demand for housing, the primary factor determining demand is the income level of the population in the market being studied. The primary reason for this is the motive of the house-buying public.

Although in many instances the rationale is used that the home is an investment, the greater majority of the population purchase homes for reasons of consumption. That is, the primary motives in home purchase are that the house under examination meets a variety of needs on the part of the family which intends to occupy it. Such factors are location to work and schools, number of rooms, baths, yard area, and a whole list of other amenities that tend to be more emotional than factual. Above all, lies the question of the monthly cost of the dwelling under question as compared to the net income of the family on a monthly basis. Indeed, the major criteria that various financial institutions look for from the family applying for a loan is whether their monthly income is adequate to meet the monthly obligations of the home purchase in question.

To state the relationship more simply: Most home buyers look at the monthly cost, and not the price of the dwelling. It has been said that any home can be sold for virtually any price, if the terms of financing were long enough and the interest low enough to make the monthly cost of occupancy low enough.

Therefore it would seem very appropriate to measure the elasticity of the demand for housing by comparing price with income. This as the basis of comparison, many researchers have found a degree of elasticity of greater than one. What this means is that the demand curve for housing is sloped at less than a 45-degree angle in the normal plotting of a demand schedule.

In terms of the functioning of the real estate market, the quite elastic demand curve for housing relative to income levels of the population means that as the price rises in terms of the burden on income, the resultant decline in the amount demanded will be greater than the price rise. Furthermore, it also implies that any sudden increase in demand will not necessarily cause a sudden leap in the price level relative to the amount demanded. These relationships are illustrated in Figure 4-13, which represents an elastic demand curve and the 45-degree slope as a reference line.

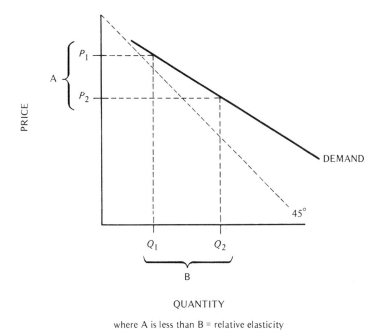

QUANTITY

where A is less than B = relative elasticity

Figure 4-13 *Relative Elasticity*

It can be seen in Figure 4-13 that no matter which force moves first, the quantity will always change in a greater amount than the amount of the relative price change. If price changes first, then the amount demanded will tend to change more drastically than the change in price. In another way, if incomes of consumers change in an appreciable manner, the demand for real estate services will tend to change even greater. If incomes drop, the decline in the demand for real estate services will incline to be greater than the income drop. If one were to be concerned with governmental action with reference to the poorly housed or the new family formations and the accommodation of such families in terms of new housing, the most direct way in which to stimulate consumption and exchange would be to address the fact that people have such low incomes relative to the costs and prices of real estate services.

THE REAL ESTATE MARKET

Now that we have studied the perfectly competitive market, and those factors that can make real estate an economic commodity, and have discussed the supply and demand characteristics of the real estate industry, perhaps it is appropriate to discuss the market structure and function in the real estate sector. It is the marketplace where the land use services are evaluated and exchanged. As a result of what occurs in that marketplace, we, as citizens, have our working and living environments altered, improved, changed, or abused. Although the real estate sector of our economy involves many different and unique segments, and local as well as national and international markets, there are some generalized traits which appear to be true to varying degrees of all markets and types of real estate services.

DISORGANIZED MARKET

The real estate market, which includes sellers as well as buyers, for the most part appears to be highly fragmented and unorganized. At any one time there are numerous sellers of various types of real property. For the most part, each seller is separated from his potential buyer. Each piece of property is totally unique and unlike nearly every other property offered for sale. The size, location, use, and characteristics of properties offered for sale are all different. Virtually none is uniform in any aspect. The largest amount of real estate activity occurs in the residential owner-occupant market, where the sellers as well as most buyers are shockingly inexperienced and uninformed.

UNKNOWLEDGABLE BUYERS
AND SELLERS

Partly because the product exchanged in the marketplace is unique in every market situation, and partly because of the infrequent entry into the market on the part of both buyers and sellers, the real estate market in the owner-occupant segment tends to involve buyers and sellers who are quite uninformed about the product they are either selling or buying. As a result of such lack of knowledge on the part of both buyers and sellers, the fair-market price of the product involved is much harder to define in terms of prices at which properties are changing hands in the marketplace. It is also partially a result of the fact that in nearly every transaction there is some degree of compulsion or distress on the part of one of the parties.

When a family sells the home it lives in, it must find another dwelling within a relatively short time. When the new resident of a community is employed in the community, he or she must find a living space relatively soon. Likewise, when people buy another dwelling somewhere in another area they are usually under some compulsion to sell the place from which they are moving. These circumstances are apt to prevail to some degree or another in nearly every transaction involving residential owner-occupant type real estate.

FEW BUYERS AND FEW SELLERS

In any specific class of property in any local market there may be few buyers of such properties in that local market, and there also may be few people in that community who are willing and actively trying to sell their properties. Under such circumstances, the few buyers and sellers active in the market are not well versed in the techniques of attracting more potential buyers or more potential properties into the area of their concern. Beyond the immediate neighborhood or peer groups, most buyers and most sellers have little across the market. The probability of these individual buyers or sellers learning what constitutes the market, and that the product is in terms of features versus what such product is really worth in the marketplace, is actually quite small.

NEED FOR PROFESSIONALS

Because the product itself is so abstract and complex in a legal and transfer sense, and because of lack of knowledge on the part of the principals in the market, the role of the professional person in the real estate field has grown tremendously over the past 50 years in the United States. Such professionalism on the part of the real estate sector has diminished—but certainly has not eliminated—the abuses and frauds that plagued the buyers and sellers of real property in the past. Nevertheless, the role of the professional in the real estate sector has tended to be confined to those areas of the market which are structured in such a manner as the owner-occupant market with the complexity, lack of knowledge, and infrequent entry and exposure on the part of the buyers and sellers who constitute that portion of the general real estate market.

PROFIT IS NOT THE MAJOR MOTIVE

One of the major reasons for the broad diversity in the product, as well as the buyers and sellers and the price fluctuations at which they arrive, is the lack of a clear-cut and measurable motive or decision-making criteria. In the decision-making process involving the transfer of owner-occupant types of property, the overriding criteria affecting the decision of purchasing is the emotional area involving personal values and tastes. Such criteria are virtually impossible to predict exactly, and therefore equally as difficult to measure. The criteria vary with the variety of people, and therefore tend to be a function of the number of persons evaluating each property type that enters the market. The fewer the observers, the less the probability that a true and fair market value was reached. Dependency such as this on the laws of probability for the fair-market value to be reached results, at least to some major extent, in the wide fluctuations in the prices at which properties change hands appear to be much alike but that the price variations would seem to dictate that they are quite different indeed.

OTHER MARKETS

As nearly all other markets involving real property are much smaller in terms of the number of transactions, they have a tendency to draw much less attention than the owner-occupant market. These other markets also tend to be established on a firmer basis in terms of the motivation and criteria employed in the evaluation and decision-making process. The first market that comes to mind would be the investment market. As the market for investment type real properties covers and includes virtually every type of property, it is commonly observable.

As with every investment vehicle, the motive in investment property is to realize a profit on the part of the owners. It may be in the operation of the property, or in holding the property until sale or transfer. In either case, the primary objective is not the occupancy and consumption of the real estate services, as is the case with residential owner-occupant previously discussed. The decison to buy or to sell property held, or to be held for investment purposes, rests in the analysis and conclusions arrived at regarding the size and profile of the profitability of the property investment. In most instances such a decision is not based on the emotions of the principals involved, but rather on a definite and measurable criteria.

Criteria such as profit is measurable in terms of money or dollars. This is also the imperfect measuring criteria employed in economic analysis. Therefore, from the economic perspective, such economic analysis will to a much more perfect degree measure and study exactly what the principles themselves are concerned about. As a result the market analysis in terms of supply and demand, and in terms of equilibrium price and quantity, is much closer to the actual market realities than perhaps would be the case in the areas and markets where the market decisions were more emotional and filled with abstract value judgments of a personal nature.

SUBSTITUTE COMPETITION

In addition the motivation of the investor group is profit and highly competitive in terms of the rate of return generated by various properties offered. Not only is the competition for investment type properties generally more intense, but the role of alternative investment vehicles is much more equal than in the consumption related to real estate purchases. In the competition for investment dollars, virtually every conceivable type of investment vehicle is in the market for such funds. The equity markets of stock and venture capital, the debt market of bonds and notes and commercial paper, as well as the various sophisticated forms of ownership interests in partnerships, syndications, and sole ownership, all are competing for the capital offered by the potential investor.

The primary reason for the widespread competition is the motivation of profit, which in itself does not reflect the physical characteristics of the investment vehicle. The criteria is much more exact in terms of liquidity, term of investment, and the very important aspect of after-tax returns to the investor. In a general way, real estate competes very favorably with such alternate forms of investments. The tax aspects of depreciation and financing, capital gains treatment, and the relatively high leverage and low downside risk, put real estate in a most favorable light in comparison with other investments.

The important aspect of the market in investment type properties is that such attractiveness is to a high degree a function of what other investments are yielding in the form of return, and also what changes in policy and law and taxes are occurring with reference to those same alternate forms of investment. The same laws and regulations which affect alternate investment forms will many times have a very dramatic impact on the real estate sector. The changes in depreciation, investment credits, and land use regulations, as well as the outright controls over rents, prices, and costs, are equally important to the investor in the real estate area when comparing such investment to what that same investor may realize in other mediums.

Finally the investment market in real property tends to be very much dominated by various expert groups which are not as dominant in the owner-occupant market. As such, the role of the real estate professional is often diminished when dealing with principals in the investment area. The principals very often have as much or more expertise in the investment area than the general real estate practitioner. The roles of accountants, consultants, lawyers, and appraisers, is much more important than is the owner-occupant who is primarily interested in occupying and consuming the real estate services he or she is contemplating to purchase.

THE REAL ESTATE MARKET AND GROWTH

The principles of economics, as related in the study or supply and demand models of the market process, are the same principles employed by the first permanent land dwellers of Jericho and the Fertile Crescent. Those individuals became permanent dwellers from the standpoint of their own evaluation of what was in their own personal best interest. The benefits of cultivation of food, or of trading and servicing traders, were greater than the alternative benefits associated with nomadic life styles. Later the benefits of living within a protective wall, and of having standing armies for mutual defense outweighed the disadvantages of having to support such public services, or of having to give gifts or sacrifices to such agents.

The later stages of moving from the country to the congested and crowded cities of the industrial era were outweighed by the benefits in the form of wages, social interaction, and common defense that such city life offered. So strong have been the individual advantages of city living, that a progressively greater proportion of the populations of the developed world are urban and city dwellers. Even in those cities that experienced a net outmigration of population in the past few years in the United States, the inhabitants for the most part moved to the fringes of the same city they had left to become part of the growing suburban population characteristic of the developed nations of the world.

It would appear that the evaluation that each individual makes in terms of the alternate advantages offered by competing life styles would nearly guarantee that the role of the city dwellers will continue to expand. In those instances where there seems to have been a sudden cohesion of motive, the result was most often the consequence of some very powerful central figure that could dictate such basic changes in life style. If we are to see any massive example of a change in the city dwelling patterns, they will most probably come from situations where the central government has made the choice one of survival or demise. Under such a choice it is in the best interest of nearly all the population to obey the directive even where it would appear to be contrary to the best economic interests of the population.

SELECTED READINGS

Carter, Harold. *The Study of Urban Geography*. London: Edward Arnold Publishers, Ltd., 1972.

Netzer, Dick. *Economics and Urban Problems*. 2nd ed. New York: Basic Books, 1974.

Perloff, Harvey S., and Lowdon Wingo, Jr. *Issues in Urban Economics*. Baltimore: Johns Hopkins University Press, 1968.

Rothenberg, Jerome. *Economic Evaluation of Urban Renewal*. Washington, D.C.: Brookings Institute, 1967.

Shafer, Thomas W. *Real Estate and Economics*. Reston, Va.: Reston Publishing Co., 1975.

Thompson, Wilbur R. *A Preface to Urban Economics*. Baltimore: Johns Hopkins University Press, 1968.

CHAPTER FIVE

ELEMENTS OF GROWTH

THE REAL ESTATE COMMODITY

The first element in the growth process is the real estate itself
and how that element functions. Unlike most other economic
commodities or services, real estate has certain unique characteristics which tend to make it behave or function differently from
most other products exchanged in the marketplace. Those characteristics most responsible for the uniqueness of real estate are:
1) the fixed location; 2) long life; 3) large economic units; and 4)
the decisions related to real estate use which are generally long-
term decisions. Let us now begin to examine each of these elements, and how they relate to the scene we have drawn of urban
growth.

Quite probably the single most important factor of the real
estate area is and always has been the fixed location of real
estate. Being fixed in one spot, real estate is either excluded from
a market or has a virtual monopoly in one market. Exclusion
results in a drastically lower value based on the reduction in the
market advantages. If a location has all the advantages of one
type of use or market, it then has far greater advantages than

most other sites and therefore can demand a much higher price in the marketplace. Such monopolies, in terms of site advantages, emerged at the very beginnings of the urbanization of mankind.

The natural advantages of the Fertile Crescent in terms of year-round agriculture generated advantages for such areas far above the advantages offered by other areas of the world. Power and wealth soon inhabited the areas of natural advantage. In later periods, advantages of a technological or transportation or political nature made certain areas also much more valuable; thus the power and wealth of those times was attracted to these newer areas. Areas such as the British Empire during the Industrial Revolution, and the United States soon afterward, illustrate these principles. More particularly, cities such as London, Liverpool, New York, Chicago, and San Francisco illustrate centers of comparative advantage which also resulted in the escalation of land prices in those areas.

In current times, as in ancient times, a very short distance can make a dramatic difference in terms of property value. A few yards outside the defensive wall of early cities was land of nearly equal character, except for the fact that it lay outside the perimeter of defense. However, being out of the defensive posture of the town or city, or kingdom, such land was much less likely to be exchanged or cultivated for extended periods of time because of the threat of destruction at the hands of some invader. In modern cities, there are somewhat similar areas whose property values have been affected by the presence of a railroad track or a bridge or a major highway, much as the fortified walk of ancient Jericho or Ur once did. This fact, that real estate must endure a location absolutely fixed in nature, has a tremendous impact on decisions relating to the property.

LONG LIFE

The fact that land has an indefinite life—or infinite life, if you prefer—and also that the man-made improvements—or distractions, if you prefer—have a very long life are factors which also weigh heavily in the use to which real estate is put. First, the knowledge that real estate tends to have such a very long life affects the decisions on the part of owners of the land. If an improvement is made, that is, if buildings or structures are erected on that real estate at that location, they will tend to remain on that land for a very long time. Once a structure is built, the very fact that it was erected eliminates the possibility of using that land for many other uses for a very long time.

This, then, tends to retard or slow down the commitment process to construction on land; and once made, it is very rarely that such improvements are changed in any drastic way for a long time. The land use patterns within cities and towns tends to be very sluggish, once improvements of a certain nature have been constructed. The only way that drastic changes in the patterns of development are apt to occur is when massive economic incentives arise that more than compensate for the lost remaining life in the improvements of a type to be changed.

The threat of condemnation by local, state, or federal government is also an incentive used in more recent times to force changes in the existing land usage of certain districts or areas within some of our cities and towns. In such cases, the economic incentives are so great in a negative way that the changes appear very good to the owners of real estate as compared to the loss of their holdings with minimal compensation. In either case, the fact that real estate has such a long life greatly contributes to the nature and the complexities of the issue.

LARGE ECONOMIC UNITS

Real estate has always exacted a high price whether in terms of monetary units, or in terms of military commitment or defense. In either case, the nature of the property rights involved have required the cooperative efforts of many people either directly or indirectly. In ancient times, the support of the military and the religious leaders was required for an estate in real property to be maintained. In more modern times the order and conduct of law, finance, and public interest have to be married together for the real property involved to be a viable economic force. The single most obvious thing about real property is that one cannot buy or acquire one square foot, or five dollars' worth of property. The units come in much larger packages, and require the accumulation of much greater wealth and/or power to enable one to acquire real estate. As a result of such a characteristic, these other areas play a very significant role in the functioning of a viable real estate market.

Because we all occupy real property in one or more ways and places, other factors play a very large part in an increasing way and in an increasing degree in all our lives. The larger the estate in real property in terms of monetary units or otherwise, the more other agents are involved in the decision-making process and the transfer and use of such property. Areas such as finance, insurance, planning, issuance of permits, and the management of real property are but a few examples of the many areas and the many people in each area that affect the entire market of real estate.

LONG-TERM DECISIONS

Finally, because of the fixed location, and the fact that real property is always a prisoner of its surroundings; because improvements in real property are longlived, which makes the costs of mistakes very high indeed; because the economic units involved are very large, and the decision-making process is virtually a consensus by committee; because of all these factors the decisions relating to the use and ownership of real property tend to be long-term decisions. Decisions are not long-term by design or intent, but rather they are long-term because they are dictated by the characteristics of the units involved. The decision-making process tends to be so drawn out, the commitments so large, and the cost of mistakes and/or changes so high, that once the miracle of decision has been made and committed, there is little prospect for the same people to back away from that decision or go through that whole process again on a property on which they have already spent a great deal of time and effort.

It therefore takes a great deal of economic incentive to persuade a large body of people involved in the decision-making process to convince them of the advantages of changing a decision once it has been made. This is also why planning without the attachment of significant economic advantage is so often a futile effort in enterprise.

THE PRINCIPALS—INDIVIDUALS

In a society so structured as the United States, where freedom of action is granted to virtually every citizen, and where the ownership of real property is open to nearly all, and the property units themselves are so broken up into small units and spread to so many individual property owners, it becomes apparent that the individual owner of property has a very great role in the decision-making process involving the use to which land and its improvements are put. Although the small single owner or investor appears not to have a great deal of latitude in the operation of the market, the role of the individual property owner in a mass of property owners does not have a great impact on the market process.

The first characteristic that becomes apparent is the tremendous degree of disorganization which tends to characterize the market in real property. There are literally millions of property owners, each owning a unique piece of property unlike the property owned by other property owners. Furthermore, the same individual is active in the real estate market at very infrequent intervals during his/her lifetime. The average life of a mortgage is something less than ten years. This implies that residential properties change hands approximately every ten years. At this rate of exchange, the average owner of real property is active in the market only four or five times in a lifetime.

Whenever one performs a task once every ten years, the ability to perform that task is not greatly enhanced during the time. In addition, the manner of performing that task may have greatly changed during the ten-year waiting span because of technology, current events, or legal changes. So it is with the operation of the real estate market, and the performance of the individuals performing within that industry. The real estate and land use sector is a dynamic environment which greatly changes from one year to the next. The world of the urban dweller changes even more dramatically because of the very nature of the urban community. Thus the knowledge on the part of individual owners and buyers of real property is diminished in its effectiveness due to the degree of inactivity that characterizes the average owner. To a large extent, this lack of knowledge accounts for the tremendous variations that prevail in the allocation process in the real estate sector. The wide range of asking and selling prices, and the wide range in the level of activity within any one area from one period to the next, very often is a result of the lack of knowledge and understanding on the part of the owners of real property. This lack of adequate current knowledge, with regard to their investments in real property, accounts to a large degree for the bulk of middlemen being in the residential property area of real estate. It also accounts for the large proportion of abuses that do occur, and tend to occur in the individual residential and speculative property areas.

THE PRINCIPALS—COMPANIES

Individual firms and business enterprises play an important role in use of real property, especially properties of a certain nature. The types of real estate most immediately associated with the decision-making processes of businesses are those properties suitable for manufacturing and commercial activities of certain types. The first general category of firms important in use of real property is that class which we shall call the owner-consumer class. Firms such as major oil and petroleum companies, steel companies, and major manufacturing industries such as autos, appliances, textiles, aluminum, shipbuilding, and many others of a similar nature, make decisions relating to real property purchase and development with reference to the suitability to their own individual needs. As a result, such firms normally maintain a sizable staff of people in a variety of disciplines which relate to and involve the various aspects of real property and the needs of that particular industry.

For example, a major oil company will maintain a staff of lawyers, appraisers, accountants, and internal people who have the function of reviewing current real estate holdings, the potential benefits or losses that would be associated with maintaining the current profile, or of the outcomes of various development alternatives. An evaluation of alternatives includes the productivity of current holdings and trends in that area, and also the searching for the best or better locations or development patterns for the future of the firm. It is no accident that Century City was a development of property of the 20th Century-Fox

Company; or that many other firms, in a variety of industries, have become major forces in the land development patterns of some of our major cities. These individual firms possess a greater knowledge of real estate, and maintain large supportive staffs that greatly aid in the decision-making process as it relates to the use and ownership of land.

In this crossover role, the owner-consumer firm reaches into the second class of company or corporation ownership which we shall call the investor-owner group. In this segment of the company ownership group the motivation on the part of the company is not to directly consume the services associated with one location, but rather to rent or lease the facilities to others who wish to utilize the advantages of those locations. In this regard, the firm is a professional investor of the highest magnitude. The important goal of the firm of this class is to accurately predict what the consumption deeds on the part of businesses of all types is going to be sometime in the future. To the extent that such a firm is correct in its predictions, it will be able to buy and develop land at a lower cost and thus realize a higher return on the investment capital than other less fortunate firms.

This professional investor class is highly sophisticated in the various techniques of investment analysis, and all the possible financing and tax advantages associated with a project being structured in various ways. Again, this class has a high level of professional expertise on its staff, which gives it a decided advantage in an industry known for its disorganization and low level of sophistication. It should also be pointed out that motives such as these firms do have are nearly totally translated into dollar return on investment or profits.

THE PRINCIPALS—GOVERNMENT

The first way in which government constitutes an element in the complex interplay of elements in the use of real estate resources is through the direct ownership of land and real property. The federal government owns a great deal of the total land area of the nation, but its ownership interests are not evenly distributed throughout the country. More than three-fourths of all the land held by the federal government is located west of the Mississippi River. Particularly along the Eastern seaboard, the amount of land area held by the federal government is quite small in relation to the proportion held elsewhere. As a result, the role of the federal government in terms of how it manages and uses its land holdings along the eastern states is much less in terms of impact than the role played by that same arm of government in other states.

It should also be pointed out that even where the federal government holds a minor amount of land in total for a given area or state, in terms of a local area or town the role of the federal government may indeed be large. A case in point would be the city of Washington, D.C., along that same eastern seaboard. The role of the federal government is nearly that of a monopolist in terms of impact within the Washington area. The decisions to build large government structures is nearly totally outside the decision process of the local area surrounding such government land holdings.

The second major area of concern in regard to the role of government at the federal level managing its land holdings, is the whole system of the federal government to allocate decisions to the agency level which often is even further removed from the citizen input into that decision-making process. In this regard one would look to the pentagon, military bases, support facilities, and a multitude of other land holdings and construction of improvements which lie far removed from the local area where the impact of such uses and abuses is apt to be the greatest.

It is also apparent that the purpose and function of such varied agencies changes with each passing election, and that there is a strong tendency for our political representatives to create committees and new agencies without an accompanying tendency to phase out or eliminate those agencies or functions of past days. The growing layers of government function also tend to delay the decision-making process as it relates to the use of lands which the government owns and occupies.

The role of state governments is very significant in regard to the way in which land use decisions are made within a state. In some states of a predominantly urban character, the role of state government is a great one in terms of the many ways in which the state is involved in the details of land transfer and use regulations. The individual states have a large role in the use and planning of real estate resources with regard to the necessary supportive services required in virtually all land use decisions in our complex and mobile society. Facilities such as roads, sewers, water, power, schools, ecology, historical landmarks, colleges, hospitals, tax base, and a multitude of other areas, are directly influenced by the actions and policies of state government. The entire system of regulation and enforcement of FHA and VA programs, although federal in nature, lies in the hands of state offices and branches of federal agencies.

The areas of subsidized housing, revenue-sharing programs, redevelopment, and urban renewal programs are closely if not entirely within the auspices of state officials. One of the largest single areas of impact on the use and patterns of development has been and continues to be the location and construction of highways and freeways. The funding of such highways programs has been mostly in a partnership between state and federal agencies.

The state agencies dictate most often the location of such systems and their construction schedule. The federal agencies are concerned mostly with the funding and operational aspects of such programs with respect to meeting the various requirements of the statute authorizing such programs.

The county and city levels of government are crucial elements in the actual land use patterns which the citizens live with, and in, each day. Through various zoning, planning, building, and other detailed departments within the structure of the counties and cities, they exert a tremendous power over the individual landowners and their desires and intentions to build or modify the physical and the use aspects of their property interests. Areas such as building permits, variances, special use permits, electrical plumbing and building inspection departments, local neighborhood, planning groups, local historical societies, and an endless list of civic interest groups are such that the individual property owner must accommodate whenever he or she desires to build, modify, or use for other purposes the real property under their ownership.

The city and county administrations also provide the local community with a variety of public services vital to the very existence of the community. Facilities such as fire and police protection, libraries, schools, water districts, sewerage districts, roads and maintenance facilities, transit facilities, entertainment centers, and a multitude of other very necessary capital investments are managed by local city and county authorities.

Probably the single most direct influence on the part of the local and county administrations is in the area of zoning. The regulation of use to which land may be put anywhere within the jurisdiction of municipal or county zoning ordinance, strikes at the very core of the process of urban land use and development. The economics of the land use decision is altered and affected in a tremendous way by the decisions made by such authorities, with reference to what is and is not a permitted use for the land resources of a specific. The decisions may be wholly within the realm of the public interest at large, and at other times it may be entirely at odds with what is the very best in the interests of the community at large and as a whole economic community. Recent policies such as "slow growth," "no growth," and "managed growth," reflect the process of the local communities flexing their political and democratic muscle in areas where they have the vested and constitutional authority to do so.

AUXILIARY FORCES

There are many other government and quasigovernment agencies which are very important in the way land use decisions are arrived at in the community at large. One of the currently growing and important powers in the land use decisions of nearly every area in all fifty states is the Environmental Protection Agency of the federal government. That agency has a tremendous amount of authority with regard to the development of land for nearly all or any purpose, from agriculture to urban growth in terms of housing or employment facilities. The Environmental Protection Agency has authority to review and deny changes in land use that would adversely affect water, land, or air quality.

The particular areas of most of the controversy have been the air and water quality aspects. Virtually any place where more than a few automobiles are grouped together, the air in that immediate area will be adversely affected. What housing development, shopping facility, or recreation facility does not have many cars and trucks associated with its location? So far, the major problem areas have been the disputes that have arisen over the scope of the authority of the EPA, and the manners in which standards have been established as the guidelines for determining the acceptable levels of change in the quality of air, water, and land. This entire area was clouded by the requirement of an environmental impact report requirement of each significant development or permit application. After such a requirement was placed on the building and development community, the facilities of the responsible agency were not yet developed to the point where they could review such reports and judge whether the applied for project approval should or should not be given.

This is but one example of an agency or law being passed which has a broad and far-reaching impact on the land use planning decisions which are being made every day. Other such areas would include the newly proposed 200-mile economic limit, tariffs and quotas on various products and services, interest ceilings, subsidy programs of various types, transportation facilities and changes, and a variety of specific laws and regulations which affect specific industries and groups in our community.

THE PRINCIPALS—BANKING

Of all the areas that affect the land use decision-making process, next to the federal and state governments, none has more complete and direct impact on real estate than the banking industry. By the banking industry we are including commercial and savings banks together, even though they are dramatically different in many ways. Referring to the factors mentioned in the previous chapter—those which tend to make real estate a unique economic commodity—one of those factors was the large economic units that real estate entails. As such, it is nearly universal for most types of real property to involve some form of debt structure.

Debt financing in real estate nearly always involves some form of banking concern. The agreement of the banks loan officer, its loan and real estate appraiser and its loan committee, significantly extends the decision-making process to include many more people than the single owner of the property. Such involvement by many more parties is quite different from the decision-making process involving other types of commodities and services traded in the market community.

In addition to the loan procedures and time extensions, the whole area of availability and cost of money is also in the hands of the banking community. The cost of financing, particularly in residential construction, is a major factor in the ability of the builder to build and sell his product in the marketplace. The characteristics of the real estate market are such that a slight rise in the interest cost involves a significant cost in terms of monthly payments and the resultant income multiple that must be met to qualify for loans of sufficient amounts to purchase homes. As a result of this quite high income elasticity of the housing demand, the costs of capital in the banking community can very quickly and dramatically affect the activity level and the allocation of real estate resources in the community, in the state, and the nation at large.

In addition, it should be remembered that the costs of money as reflected in interest rates may have very little to do with the level of incomes in the same city, state, or country as a whole. The rates charged to borrow money in the marketplace are ever changing in response to changes in demand and supply of money in the week-to-week and month-to-month time frame.

This leads us into the next segment of the economy which has a very high impact on the real estate market, and that is the financial community at large. This sector would include institutional investors and lenders, the stock and equity markets, the debt markets, the flow of funds nationally and internationally, the fiscal policy on the part of the United States government and others, as well as the international monetary system, and the trading profile of the United States economy.

First, it should be realized that the real estate community does not occupy a vacuum it alone may fill. The entire real estate community operates within a dynamic and complex economy that constantly interacts one part with another. As a result of this close interaction, what is happening in one sector has an effect on the activities of those in other sectors. What this means is that where the returns are very high in secure investment and debt instruments, the resultant activity in the real estate sector will tend to decline as it will not be able to offer as high, or as liquid, or as secure investments at or near the returns being realized in those other markets.

When this phenomenon is confined to the savings and loan industry it is referred to as "disintermediation." What happens is that monies on deposit in savings institutions are withdrawn and deposited or invested in higher-yielding secure investments in bonds or other high-grade instruments of equal character but greater liquidity. In such a case the available funds in the savings industry are decreased, and the result is that there is less available money for home buyers to borrow at reasonable rates and terms. The cost of financing rises, and therefore the real cost of home occupancy is also raised. As the price goes up in real terms, the potential market in which to sell such a product diminishes.

In this way it can be seen that the very complex world of finance and money management has an important and direct impact on the state of affairs in the real property field. It should also be acknowledged that the rates of return realized in the various areas of finance have a dramatic impact on the amount of investment capital available to the real estate sector. As the vacancy rates decline in the real property sector, the earnings on the part of owners of real property tend to rise.

Such a rise, when it exceeds what is available in other forms of investments, tends to attract capital into the real estate sector. The opposite effect is realized when other sectors are more prosperous, or when the supply and demand conditions in real estate act in such a manner as to lower the rates of return because of higher vacancies or much higher operating costs.

Another impact of the financial sector on the real property use part of the economy is the impact on the real estate community when one or more sectors of the financial community have serious problems. The recent success of the Real Estate Investment Trusts (REITs) culminated in a sharp decline and deterioration of earnings, and indeed many actually were forced to declare bankruptcy. There was great reluctance on the part of many in the financial community to advance funds for sound and well researched and planned developments that were badly needed by the consumers of housing the nation. Furthermore, the losses were so large and so widespread that the very financial strength of many of our lending institutions was in question and remains so to this time.

Another example of an important element of the financial community with regard to the health and smooth operations in the real estate sector is the area of mortgage underwriting. For many years the FHA was the only agency around to underwrite the mortgages issued by the various lenders. In the early 1960s the first private mortgage insurance firm was established and began to offer its services. Since the early 1970s, when major government agencies in the secondary mortgage markets began to accept mortgages underwritten by private as well as government insurance plans, private insurance policies began to really establish themselves as a viable force in the financial community.

Although still nearly totally a service provided to the lending community at their request, the private mortgage insurance by its very nature encourages those same lenders to lend money to purchasers of real property that they may not be so willing to lend without any reduction in the risk of exposure. In this way the presence of the private mortgage insurance industry creates the potential money available to underwrite the transactions which occur within the real estate sector.

The introduction of the Electronics Funds Transfer system (EFT) in the most recent years, which has yet to be fully established, shows another very big evolution in the financial and trading communities. This system is based on the concept that an account may be credited or debited through the use of electronics rather than requiring the issuing, handling, and endorsing of checks and money orders. The result of shifting these activities to the speed of computer technology is to drastically reduce the handling and processing time required for the more normal money transfers between buyers and sellers. The reduction in transfer time allows transactions to be made and completed much more quickly.

The biggest advantage to the money markets of the world, as well as the single nation, is the reduction in the total amount of money constituting the "float"—money floating between accounts in the process of transfer amounts to many millions of dollars which are not and cannot earn a return through use. By reducing that amount of float in a significant way, or entirely, more money in our economic system can be used for useful purposes. The speed of transactions to completion, and the virtual elimination of the money float, are significant benefits offered by the EFT systems now being developed.

SELECTED READINGS

Barlowe, Raleigh. *Land Resource Economics.* 2nd ed. Englewood Cliffs, N.J.: Prentice-Hall, 1972.

James, Franklin L., and James W. Hughes. *Economic Growth and Residential Patterns.* New Brunswick, N.J.: Center for Urban Policy Research, Rutgers University, 1972.

Mills, Edwin S. *Urban Economics.* Glenview, Ill.: Scott, Foresman and Co., 1972.

Reid, Margaret C. *Housing and Income.* Chicago: University of Chicago Press, 1962.

Shafer, Thomas W. *Real Estate and Economics.* Reston, Va.: Reston Publishing Co., 1975.

Smith, Halbert C., et al. *Real Estate and Urban Development.* Homewood, Ill.: Richard D. Irwin, Inc., 1973.

Weimer, Arthur M., et al. *Real Estate.* 6th ed. New York: Ronald Press, 1972.

Wingo, Lowdon, Jr. *Cities and Space.* Baltimore: Johns Hopkins University Press, 1963.

PART THREE

GROWTH–WHAT IS IT?

So far, the subject of growth has been raised throughout much of the discussion. It is appropriate at this point to examine the definition of that term, and come to some agreement on what the concept of growth means or should mean. It is a fundamental part of the subject of urbanization that compels us to be concerned with the uses to which land area under examination is put; therefore we will also examine the concept of land use, and the various methods by which we control and determine the use of real property.

It is also a very integral part of the urbanization process that such processes are influenced and controlled by the controls over land use. These controls over land use include a variety of private as well as public powers and instruments. So we will also discuss and examine those controls and their economic impact in the marketplace for real property.

CHAPTER SIX

A REDEFINITION
OF GROWTH

THE CONCEPT OF GROWTH

In the previous chapter we have seen that there are many ways to observe or define what we mean by growth. In the urban environment we often use the term growth to imply an increase in the number of inhabitants in a subject area or city; we also see the concept implied to mean an increase in everything associated with the urban scene. Fundamentally, we are concerned with the manner in which people use and consume the real estate services of an area or city. What was suggested as a possible concept of growth was the magnitude and process of change in the intensity with which people use the available real estate resources of an area.

This shifting toward a greater intensity of land use, which resulted in a greater productivity of the land mass involved, was the basis of the concept of growth in the economic sense. The land use decisions made by the individuals involved is the fundamental part of the growth equation that has so far eluded discussion. Since the individuals make up the entire market of the economic model, what tends to make most persons choose city life over the life style offered by the rural areas? What basic drives motivate such a priority system?

MOTIVATION OF THE INDIVIDUALS

Based on well documented experience with fellow human beings, we have assumed that most of the time most people will prefer to maximize their economic benefits rather than diminish or stagnate them. Such economic measures that do exist are more consequence than cause. One thing that must be logically inferred is that motivation of groups or individuals is founded in the results of such action fulfilling some needs within those same individuals. Although we must recognize from the outset that all individuals are unique in many respects—just as every parcel of real property is unique—all human beings have a great number of factors and basic needs in common.

Just as each family has its own manner of satisfying its housing needs, and will tend to choose different styles and types of homes, all homeowners have the fact of home ownership preference in common. Although each is unique, all together they represent the owner-occupant market we have studied. Likewise, each human being has certain basic human needs that each will fulfill in his or her own unique way. Those basic needs are present in nearly all human beings, and so we may also generalize about them just as we did about the owner-occupant market.

We therefore come to a restatement of the preference for city life over rural life as expressed by the majority of persons in the developed world. What is it that city life offers in the terms of need fulfillment, which the rural life tends not to fulfill for the majority of people?

MASLOW'S NEEDS HIERARCHY

As A. H. Maslow postulated in his text, *Motivation and Personality*, in 1954, human beings of all types have basic needs common to all other human beings. Maslow classified these needs as five basic levels of needs.

The first was physiological needs, those basic physical needs for physical survival. The second class of needs were those associated with safety and security. The third level of basic needs was occupied by needs of a social nature, needs of affiliation and acceptance. The fourth level of needs was that related to the individual's ego and reputation or prestige. The highest level of need satisfaction was described as those needs on the part of a person to do that which he or she is good at doing.

When people seemingly have reached the very heights of success and achievement they very often become equally as inspired at climbing mountains, sailing ships, or raising horses for purposes that appear to be totally personal. Such needs for self-fulfillment and self-actualization would occupy the highest level of the need hierarchy. Such ordering of the basic needs of the human being seems, to this student, as being totally within the realm of possibility. Although from an individual and personal basis one may argue that such generalizations about human behavior is too general and too vague to be of any real use, it would appear that the application of such a ladder of progression of need satisfaction would greatly explain the way in which groups of human beings seem to function over time in the urbanization process.

PHYSIOLOGICAL NEEDS

Apparently the initial steps toward urbanization were made on the basis of very basic natural advantage of one area over another in terms of such an area to provide food and shelter on a year-round basis. The ability or opportunity to fulfill the food needs of a human being without the enduring threats of travel were undoubtedly the first motivating factors in the initial stages of city growth. It would indeed seem that such early and basic advantages are exactly what accounts for nearly all city formation in the early stages.

The discovery of gold, oil, a new port, rich interior of agricultural lands, a shipping point or railhead, a resort town or community, it would appear that all were initially established on the premise that one could survive and earn a living in such places and somehow better than the physical satisfaction of basic needs which other areas may have provided.

SAFETY AND SECURITY NEEDS

Industrial societies maintain community standards of social programs that tend to establish acceptable levels of poverty, or sickness, or education which are inclined to be much lower than the acceptable levels of such handicaps in rural areas. The major reason is that the concentrated wealth of the cities and urban areas has within its power the ability to do something about unemployed workers, epidemics of illnesses of various kinds, hospitals, and even schools, if only for the wealthier children. The major security factors of the cities were the larger employment bases and the growing economical bases of such cities, which tended to assure everyone of a job sooner or later. If one job was lost due to company or personal failure, the city offered the prospect of another.

Additionally, in the early stages of city formation the maintaining of a garrison was very much a factor in the safety and security of the inhabitants of such a city. Europe, Mesopotamia, the Fertile Crescent, and more recently the American West, all witnessed the development of city forts. Even today many of the developed cities of the world are dominated by military structures of one type or another. Such safety and security as these cities offered was very much a factor of the development of cities at a time in human history when security and survival in the physical sense were a very large concern in the day-to-day lives of most citizens.

SOCIAL NEEDS

The need of all human beings to associate with other human beings is the basis of the social class of needs in the needs hierarchy. More than mere association with other human beings, however, the social needs are more in the area of association with other people of similar nature, values, religion, needs, aspirations, work, education, wealth, or other major interest category. The tendency of professional persons to live and work within close proximity of one another, or of industrial workers to live in similar areas, is reflective of this social need.

The areas of purely social activities tend to demonstrate

this social affiliation even more. There are certain types of entertainment, places of entertainment; and it is the same with sports which reflect, on the whole, one social class of people from another. It is not merely the money involved that determines such social classes or affiliations, but rather the acceptance of the established group of a new member of certain station in a social definition that determines the presence of such classes.

The ability to understand and be competent in bridge, checkers, poker, chess, lawn tennis, or lawn bowling, is not the primary criterion in becoming a member of a social club of a certain sector in the community, but rather having some common interests and values with the other members of such a club that appears to be the major criterion.

Beyond the individual, we have the same general class of motivational factors playing a part in the directions which communities and cities and even nations take over time. As a community becomes more affluent in terms of fulfilling the other more basic needs, then that community comes as the next higher level of need satisfaction on the part of the members of that community as a whole. Although not all members of a community may have substantially satisfied the lower needs, the majority of the community has. At this point the community may develop civic pride, and attempt to bind its citizens together in comparison with other communities. It then begins to develop a social consciousness that results in some of the more social programs which generally benefit the citizens of the community although not the majority.

Things such as civic activities of social and benevolent nature that draw state, regional, or national attention, tend to be directly beneficial to only two groups: Those that promote and are active in the activity, and those that receive some of the benefits from such programs. The majority of citizens are not direct beneficiaries of such programs. The growth in the pride of community can also be seen in the elevation of the educational system of the region above that of other regions. Although such indicators are taken to mean that the community benefits from the better educational system, empirical evidence has been hard put to establish a direct and measurable cause-and-effect relationship. The growing from a class neighborhood or community of similar income, education, and status in the social sense, to the sometimes pretentious and often public-relations oriented social activities calendar, is very often more reflective of the ego level of the community identified than the social level of interaction on the part of the citizens of that same community.

Such phrases as "Biggest Little City in the World," "America's Finest City," "Hometown USA," and the " 'XXXX' Capital of the World," are all indicative of the ego class of need fulfillment that communities, states, and even nations can develop. It is helpful, from the point of view of the student of urban development and trends, to observe the activities of levels such as these as a general guide into the level of need satisfaction at which such communities are operating.

Finally there is the highest level of need satisfaction, and that is the self-fulfillment level. This level of need is purely individual in terms of what satisfies such needs. There are, however, some indications of areas of communities which tend to reflect such levels on the part of their citizens. The community of wealth and affluence that tends to place a very high premium on privacy and leaves its citizens alone with a minimum of social programs of a community nature would seem to reflect a population living at or near the highest level of needs. Most often, of course, if an individual is living at this level of need satisfaction, that person's world is a small and quite private one. The nature of such personal needs is inclined to be very private and involves few other people. The artist, writer, poet, sculptor, each seems to be very much a private person most of the time. Therefore a community dominated by such types would likewise tend to be personal in its life style and character rather than social or event-oriented.

FUNCTIONING OF THE NEEDS HIERARCHY

In the process of fulfilling the needs in the order outlined, each of us will fulfill our needs to a substantial level or degree prior to going on to the next level of needs. How we fulfill those needs is a very personal thing; but the fact that we do fulfill them to a high degree before going to the next level is characteristic of most human beings. What this implies is that what motivates human beings depends on what level people are at in terms of the hierarchy of needs. Now the important thing is that whenever a threat occurs to a lower-level need that has been substantially satisfied, then that person, or that community, or that nation will tend to react in a direct and immediate manner. We may be at the level of need satisfaction that social programs are very prominent. They may be strong movements in the areas of minimum wages, higher standards of health for all persons, greater education benefits for all people, and much more livable retirement programs for those beyond certain ages.

No one would argue long on a philosophical point that such programs were not morally good and beneficial to society. But given a sudden downturn in economic events where unemployment is very high, and savings and security are very much in jeopardy, such social programs, no matter how good and how moral, will tend to disappear very quickly. Does this mean that such programs are no longer needed? Certainly not. They would probably be needed more than before. The population has suddenly been brought down in terms of the hierarchy of needs to a lower level of needs.

Under such depressed economic conditions as have been outlined, most of the population would be quickly brought to the physical survival and safety levels of need satisfaction. It would make little difference where that population was before the turn in economic events; they now are operating at the very basic and fundamental levels of needs satisfaction.

SOCIAL AND NEED PARAMETERS

It should also be kept in mind that as one moves progressively up to higher need levels, the area or geographical world of which the satisfaction of that next higher need is a part also expands. The primary needs of food and shelter are very local in character. These needs are generally satisfied mostly within the immediate area in which an individual is present. As the social and ego needs become predominant, the geographical or physical world that satisfies them expands beyond the immediate area in which the individual resides. Examples would be the social recognition that comes from being the strongest man or the best cook, which progressively involves a larger area of comparison as the individuals involved dominate their local communities. They then move on to become or to vie for the strongest man in the state or country, the best cook in the state, and so on.

Social needs tend to be fulfilled within the confines of one's job or vocation and at the local region or community level. Club membership and society pages generally reflect a very local social system of identification. At the ego level of needs, however, the comparison soon involves entire industries, or countries; and in the cases of some international sports and activities, the entire world. A world champion is the height of ego fulfillment in those areas that subscribe to such identification. The wealthiest, or the brightest, are also often involved in an international comparison.

In the case of communities of people, the same types of comparisons are made. Any local chapter of a city or state chamber of commerce, or a tourist bureau, offers quick examples of the types of fulfillment which deal with the ego levels of need satisfaction. Things such as civic pride and character are founded mostly in the area of ego reinforcement for a community at large. Things such as architecture theme development and maintenance, as well as aesthetic aspects of the local community, are reflective of the types of things which reflect the ego need level in a community's level of need satisfaction.

This does not mean that all citizens of a community are substantially satisfied in regard to the needs at the lower levels. What it does imply is that the majority of the population of such a community are substantially satisfied in terms of the needs at the lower levels.

CHANGE IN NEED PRIORITY

An example of the change that can occur in the need priorities of a community, or even an entire nation, would be in the area of environmental concerns. There is little doubt that most, if not all, Americans are very concerned about the world in which they live. Given the choice between a clean open environment and a smoggy polluted one, all people would be inclined to choose the clean environment. But when the population is living at a time of growing prosperity, people will more likely choose to bear the expense of cleaning up past damage. When a sudden downturn in economic activity occurs after such a choice has been made, the downturn jeopardizes need satisfactions at a much lower level of needs.

The difference between social problems, or even self-fulfillment, and the needs associated with physically surviving and providing for one's family is a great gap indeed! The sudden shift to a lower level of need satisfaction will tend to take priority over any and all decisions made while at a higher need level. In the middle 1970s, a case in point was the environmental strip-mining regulations passed to repair and protect the environment from the consequences of strip-mining. As soon as the price of oil imports went up significantly, and the cost of fuel in general was much higher, and at the same time there was a slowing down of the economy with its rise in unemployment, great pressure was placed on the political lawmakers of the national government to back away from some of the very good environmental protection laws. The major reason for this retreat was that such laws were partly responsible for the low coal production and high cost of fuel.

What happened was that a very significant portion of the population had found itself shifting from a socially conscious need level back to a more immediate and important need level of economic survival and the immediate benefit to themselves and their families. As a result, the strip-mining bill was delayed by the President for several years to prevent the cost of energy from rising far above what the general population could comfortably endure.

SPECIFIC INDUSTRY SECTORS

OWNER-OCCUPANT

The needs hierarchy, when applied to the owner-occupant market, tends to explain for what type of home such people will be in the market. It will also tend to define what characteristics will be most important to those in the owner-occupant market. The classic example has been the migration of the immigrants from the inner city out to the suburbs as their incomes and social acceptance improved over time.

In the lower income groups, the need for housing is met in the most economical fashion. The people are generally not beyond the safety level of need satisfaction, and many are still in the physical need level. As such, the price of a dwelling is the primary factor. They already know that in all probability they are not able to afford the size of housing facility they require. It usually settles down to getting anything or the maximum they can get for the little amount they have to spend. At the middle class level of society they tend to be operating at a social or ego level of need satisfaction. As such, they tend to seek dwelling space amongst their peers.

We begin to see class neighborhoods develop from the position of choice on the part of the persons occupying them, rather than the class of imposed neighborhoods which the poorer population does not inhabit by choice. At the upper ends of the middle-class income levels, the signs of ego satisfaction begin to appear. The swimming pools, the country estates, the mini-ranches and ranchettes, and bonus or game rooms, are examples of amenities that tend to reflect ego satisfaction rather than lower-level needs.

At the highest levels of the middle class and the lower levels of the upper-income levels we begin to see a strong preference for location in certain areas no matter what the physical characteristics of the land in question. The desire to establish oneself in a certain area of upper-income residents is likely to reflect the ego of the buyer. The concept of wanting to know "I have arrived" is very often on the minds of the first-time residents of the higher income and more prestigious communities. Things such as having a very large home with only two people living in it is not uncommon in those areas. The extreme examples of ego fulfillment would lean toward homes in the million-dollar price ranges and the estates and castles on the Continent. The huge amount of entertaining done by many such owners again tends to reflect the ego reinforcement judgment. In these cases, price is secondary to the address and the size and complexity of the amenities offered.

One final comment about the owner-occupant market should be made. In this market, more than perhaps any other, there is a very strong resistance to retracting to a lower level. In many cases such persons will try to cut back on nearly everything else before retreating to a lower level of home in terms of size and social status location. It is, I suppose, almost the same as admitting that one was not capable of living there in the first place, or of resisting the admission that their fortunes had passed. However, it is a characteristic of the owner-occupant market that upward mobility is much more fluid than the downward mobility of the same people.

INVESTMENT MARKET

The motivation on the part of the investment community is predominantly one of profit. As such, there is apt to be much less emotion involved in a market of this kind. The ability to change directions from an investment point of view is much greater than in the consumption oriented markets. Therefore one may find a smoother transition process on the part of individual investors from one investment vehicle to another. Although real estate as an investment has a very strong disadvantage in terms of its liquidity, there still tends to be a smoother buying and selling process in that market.

In terms of the motivation of investors as a group, the primary motivation in ownership of various investment vehicles remains in the form of profit. Money return on invested dollars may confine itself to the second level of primary needs if one can at all classify such motivation in terms of the basic need structure outlined. As such, the reaction on the part of individuals to changes in the investment picture are generally quick and very strong. Other needs in the social, ego, and self-fulfillment areas might be satisfied through means other than investing the types of real estate holdings. No doubt that ego has been a large part of many investors' motivation; most such bases of decision-making in the investment area have led investors astray from sound analytical judgment.

COMMERCIAL AND INDUSTRIAL CONSUMPTION

Primarily because of the scale of such projects in terms of economic commitment, investments are not quickly changed. In terms of the location of a plant, or of an office structure, the business involved could endure a downturn in the market of their product or service to the point where the actual survival of such firms is in question. Then, as a result of thorough analysis of asset management and cash flow profile the firm may indeed back away from a major capital plant or structure because of the economic considerations involved. Again, the rational is profit and not social, ego, or self-fulfillment. Although advertising and public image may well be factors inhibiting the quick change from such a commitment, ultimately the decision rests in terms of cash flow and the market being lost or gained as a result.

Established firms of sound financial strength will sometimes find themselves in the position of lacking adequate social acceptance of their firm or industry. Given a sound financial base, such firms will often construct facilities in locations in the architectural style that pure profit motivation in the short perspective would dictate otherwise. It is the difference between the short-term versus the long-term perspective. The long-term profitability of the firm may well be enhanced through the commitment to social and community causes at the cost of immediate profits. The primary motivation on the part of such a firm is the profitability of the firm over the future, and such social and community acceptance of the firm will tend to lead to acceptance of that firm's ideas, products, and services also in the future.

BEHAVIORISM AND REAL ESTATE

Currently there are many developing concepts and studies on the motivation and behavior of the human species. The basic concept of Maslow discussed in this chapter is only an introduction. The study of human behavior may yet lead us to other concepts more pragmatically related to market behavior of groups of people. The ideas involving different factors of motivation, depending on which direction one is moving in the needs hierarchy, has been developed by F. W. Herzberg and others.

The concept that human motivation may be filtered or altered based on the individual's perception of his or her ability or likelihood of success has been developed by Victor Vroom. These are only three of the many people studying human behavior, and these studies may well prove to be of extreme value in the sphere of economics and the market process involving the trend of urbanization. In the study of real estate, or urban land use, or economics, we must keep in mind that we are studying human beings and the consequences of their decision-making. The importance of the economic definition of growth.

Although there are many different ways to define growth, the most logical in terms of the history of urbanization has been a definition centered around the principles of economics. The beginnings of urbanization were based upon the inherent agricultural and trade advantages of certain areas and locations. The continued growth of urbanization through the past 10,000 years has been caused by economic self-interest more than any other single cause.

In the current stage of economic development, the developed world has nearly universally reached a point of social or governmental planning to continue and promote the growth of the more simple past. In this atmosphere of central and government planning at various levels it is very easy for such detached levels of human experience to become divorced from the operational world of economics and the direct allocation of scarce resources. Whatever the role of the government planning agencies may be, and no matter what their central theme of concern may be, it is of most importance for such agents to maintain their plans in an economic light. The object of such plans should be, and indeed must be to survive, founded upon the economic strengths of adaption of such plans.

Maslow and other human behaviorists have shown that all human beings have the same major categories of needs which they seek to fulfill in their individual manner. The major point in such theories as Maslow's is that such needs are really a series of motivational levels. Each need level tends to be fulfilled or motivating after the previous levels of needs have been substantially fulfilled. Economics as a broad body of need-satisfying entities reaches from the very basic survival and safety needs through the social and ego needs of all human beings. Such strong and broad motivation as the economic sphere presents has proven such economic motivation to be a very positive form of causation in the determination of growth and living patterns of peoples throughout the world and throughout the history of urbanization.

Finally, the concept of growth as we have discussed it in terms of change in land use and the intensity of land use is a fact of human existence. That is to say, we must entertain the concept of continual and ever growing growth. Without changes in land use there is mere existence through stagnation. As the world and humanity change and grow, the use of land within the populated areas of the world must likewise grow and change. In the absence of such accommodation on the part of a people or nation to the demands of changing land use and growth, an area and its economy soon become stagnant.

Stagnation of a local economic system soon leads in turn to the decline of commercial and trading intercourse with other communities of man. In the absence of trade and the activity and development that result from such trading, any nation or economy soon becomes a closed system producing only enough for its own consumption. Under such a closed system the development of technology and mental advancement of mankind soon bypass such a community. The result then is a declining society. Such gradual decline as the Greeks and the Romans or sudden fall such as the Czars and the Kaiser lead to the eventual replacement of such stagnated societies with new social structures that are more adept at accommodating the concept of economic growth.

Ultimately then, the lack of embarrassing growth results in stagnation and decline. The end result is that for a community or nation to survive it must understand and nurture growth through change. Nothing is more vital to developed areas, urban communities, and those areas and peoples aspiring to become developed than the concept of growth and the conditions that encourage and guide such growth.

SELECTED READINGS

Maslow, A. H. *Motivation and Personality*. New York: Harper and Brothers, 1954.

Richards, Max D., and Paul S. Greenlaw. *Management: Decisions and Behavior*. Homewood, Ill.: Richard D. Irwin, 1972.

Vroom, Victor H. *Work and Motivation*. New York: John Wiley and Sons, 1964.

PART FOUR

THE USE OF LAND

Urbanization actually is nothing more than the change in the way we normally use the land. It is a change from the extractive use of land in the form of agriculture to the more intense ways of using land resources such as in trade and commerce. The following chapters discuss land use in more exact detail.

Chapter 7 concentrates on the theories of land use and the various land use patterns that have developed through history. The fundamenal concepts of comparative advantage, continuous site competition, principle of proportionality, and the concept of highest and best use are covered in detail.

Chapter 8 focuses attention on the concepts of land use planning and the controls over land use. The legal system and the various elements of governmental sector as they relate to and control land use are discussed. The subtle impact of ownership of land on the part of the public as well as private sectors is also covered. Finally, the economic impact and the implications of such planning and controls are discussed.

CHAPTER SEVEN

LAND USE PATTERNS AND THEORY

That there are nearly as many patterns of land use and city layout as there are cities and towns seems to be very obvious when one looks at the multitude of cities and towns at his or her disposal. However, in a general sort of way there appear to be several similarities in the towns and cities one observes. It is the strong similarities that led to the development of various theories of land use patterns. That there are strong similarities in the patterns of land use in most cities in the world should not come as a surprise, since the forces which lead to urbanization generally seem to be the same forces everywhere. Cities everywhere tend to have certain characteristics that smaller and more rural communities do not have.

CITY CHARACTERISTICS

As E. W. Burgess pointed out (7:48–52) most cities have a greater number of women than men as compared to rural areas. Whatever the causes of such an occurrence, the rigid rules of men and women in the past have had a dramatic impact on the character of a city of such a characteristic as that. More women in the past generally meant a lower proportion of the population being employed. Even today such a characteristic would imply a lower total take-home wage than if as many men were present in the labor force as in rural areas. Also there are apt to be more young people and more old persons than in the rural areas. These groups tend to be more dependent on others for their well-being and existence than the middle groups. There also are more foreign-born in cities than in rural areas. This is due primarily to the nature of cities to be major ports of trade, and thus the first stopping point for those who come to a country for the very first time. Again, the marginal participation in the indigenous culture is inclined to make these people less able to live and earn a suitable living in terms of employment than others in the society.

The assimilation of the foreign-born is a slow process for most cultures, and one in which the first generation generally must pay a high price in terms of low income and marginal or low levels of material well-being. Finally, most cities are frequently characterized as having a more varied or heterogeneous selection of viable occupations than can be found in the rural areas if not in all countries. With these characteristics as a background, and remembering the inherent economic advantages of city living versus rural life, we now turn to some of the theories of land use patterns which have been developed.

THE RING OR CIRCLE PATTERN

In Figure 7-1 is depicted the concept of the circle or ring land use patterns that have been seen in some cities in the nation. The original city was formed around the trading docks or port in (1). As the city began to grow and prosper it moved outward from that point to (2). In many of our older cities some of the evidence of such staged development is still there for observation. The major industrial and business activities remained in (1); but the residential uses moved out of town for the privacy and safety in terms of traffic and noise that (2) offered. Additionally, area (2) also had the open land area required of the larger estates which the successful members of the business community were moving out of the city proper to build.

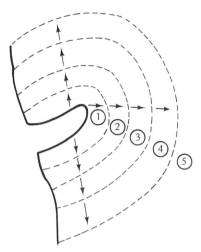

Figure 7-1 *Concentric Ring Pattern*

Over time, and as the industrial and manufacturing activities began to expand, area (2) began to be the primary housing area for the large populations of working peoples the Industrial Revolution required. It was not long before area (2) began to contain mostly working-class people, who preferred that area because of its close proximity to the industrial plants. The growing middle class then moved a bit farther out into (3) where the lots and homes were bigger and cleaner than in the inner city areas of (2) and the industrial sector of (1).

The advent of adequate transportation facilities also made the move out to the fringes of the older parts of the city possible and feasible for those who could afford such facilities. It was common to see the second and third generation immigrants that had now become established parts of the society and culture of the United States moving into these newer suburbs. The outer parts of the city were now the sites of the higher income communities which were often surrounded by farming areas and recreational areas; (4) and (5) represent the agricultural parts of the land use picture, with (4) being the high-income horse-and-estate set, with some small farms and truck farms in the area. Part (5) is the open land of farming and forest areas that are the future victims of this circle-sprawl type of land usage.

The important part of this theory is that each inner circle zone may at nearly all times be putting pressure on the next outer zone for its residents and the land use they represent. The industrial and business community of (1) as it becomes successful and continues to grow will in all probability take over more of zone (2). The low-income residents comprising the majority of land usage in area (2) will be putting pressure on the residents of zone (3) for more space. Area (3) may then exert pressure on area (4), and area (4) will tend to progressively consume more of the land area in zone (5).

This has been referred to as the filtering process in land use, where the homes of the middle and upper class of today become the homes of the lower and lower-middle class tomorrow. As new homes are built and sold, the old homes are apt to become the homes of those who previously could not afford to live in such areas or size of home. This same filtering process occurs in other types of real estate uses, where the older homes become shops and boutiques as the business area expands outward into formerly residential sections.

RADIAL CORRIDOR THEORY

The radial corridor theory of land use is based on the observation that development appears to take place along major transportation routes both in and between cities. Within a city such corridors are usually roads and bus routes. It also may be seen along railroad and water transportation routes where there are frequent stops and relatively slow-moving traffic. From the major business district there extend arms of business and development parallel to and along the major transportation routes.

In Figure 7-2, the central business and industrial area is depicted as (1). From that core area, businesses of a separate type tend to locate along the transportation route. Generally these are businesses of a retail and service nature rather than manufacturing and commerce, as in the central city core. The next area of land use type is usually the multifamily residential and transient residential, as depicted in area (3). The lower-income working population locates in these areas because of the lower residential land rents, and because of the close proximity to public and private transportation facilities into the core area of manufacturing and commerce. The middle-class income population tends to locate in the next area (4) which is further removed from the busy commercial and industrial areas, but remains close enough to corridors for transportation and facilities of a public nature, such as hospitals, schools, libraries, and public transportation.

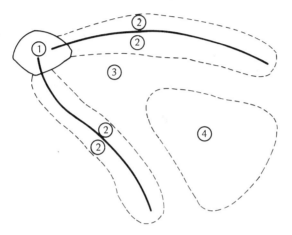

Figure 7-2   *Radial Corridor Pattern*

In area (5) are located the higher-income residential areas as well as the rural or open spaces which provide seclusion and privacy not to be found in the majority of other closer areas. As in the circle theory of land use, the pressure of each area extends into the next area so long as the community is growing and is productive. Therefore it is quite common to see the development of industrial parks, financial districts, educational complexes, medical service facilities, and retail shopping complexes of sizable proportions, develop in the areas of (3), (4), and even (5) on occasion.

The fundamental difference in the radial corridor theory is that one of the major determinants in the patterns of land use within a community is the location of major roads and transportation facilities. The decision-making process that takes place with reference to the location of these facilities is a conscious effort on the part of the citizens of that community. Thus the importance of such decision-making by selected individuals is of fundamental importance to the extent that the radial corridor theory is accurate in describing the land use patterns of a community.

MULTIPLE NUCLEI THEORY

In the multiple nuclei theory of land use patterns there are several enclaves of specific use—or predominantly one use—which are connected to the central business area by major transportation routes. Such individual centers are connected to the central economic forces of the community by major transportation routes that traverse areas of no or little development at all. Areas between the centers may in fact be agriculture, but in the majority of cases it is merely vacant land. Land of this kind is often held for speculation that its value will increase over time as it becomes more appropriate for another use. Figure 7-3 illustrates the multiple nuclei theory of land use.

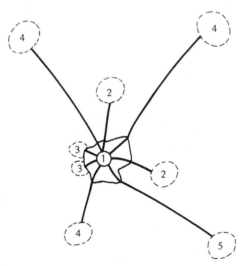

Figure 7-3 *Multiple Nuclei Pattern*

Area (1) would tend to be the major economic area of the community. It may be trade, commerce, manufacturing, or a number of other activities; however, it remains very securely tied to that location. Not far from such an area may be some of the other businesses of the community of an unlike nature. These other businesses would not be compatible with the basic industry of the area, but may indeed be very important to the economic health of an area. Facilities such as major research and educational complexes with high technology industry located quite close would be an example of business use as it is depicted in area (2). Military establishments are another example of the type of economic facilities basic to an area but are most often divorced from the economic activities of the community itself.

Frequently the next enclave of specific use is the residential area for the lower-income population, although in some areas it may indeed be a high-income and well established and tradition-filled area. An area such as this is depicted by the (3) circles. Such use is many times very close to the central business area and generally easily identifiable as a separate area altogether. The middle class also tends to live in areas easily distinguishable from others in the community or area. They are often identified as very large and recently developed areas of homes, schools, parks, and some small retail and service uses. Finally, the higher-income groups also tend to have their separate areas of residence where virtually all the homes in that area are expensive relative to the homes in the other areas.

Although it is somewhat easier to maintain an area that is separated from other uses, the various nuclei do tend to extend their land usage to other uses partly due to the needs of the individuals in the community for retail and service type businesses, also because of some pressure in recent years exerted by federal and state governments to make their communities more open to varying economic backgrounds—implied and even stated pressure in some cases to make such nuclei more heterogeneous in terms of the ethnic and cultural composition of the residents.

The major thrust of the study of this type of land use theory is to raise the question of the purpose of transportation routes. There is little doubt that transportation systems representing capital outlays and investment by the community at large are a key element in the success or failure of land development and land use changes. The important question is whether such transportation location decisions should precede development, or fill the needs of the population that has already moved to such a location. There is little doubt that where major roads do not appear, often there is extreme pressure by special groups to have the transportation planners and politicians allocate enormous funds for this road or that. The result of this will be enormous gains in value for those landholders in such areas that are intent upon developing or holding for speculation the land areas in question.

The transportation authorities are under a great deal of pressure from the public at large to lower the cost of transportation construction. In so doing, the easiest way is to purchase and build roads where there are not yet any people. That decision then becomes the major decision in terms of determining for certain where such development will occur in the future.

THE SECTOR THEORY

Homer Hoyt developed the sector therapy as an explanation or a description of the land use patterns of developed cities (6:276–77). The basic concepts of the sector are outlined in Figure 7-4. Each body of people may segregate itself on the basis of income and social position. This self-imposed type of segregation tends to establish areas within a city of identifiable income and social classes. Members of such an income or social class may live and associate with others of that same income and social class. In observing a community, one may be able to identify geographical sectors where the inhabitants of each sector are different and separate from members of other sectors.

Furthermore, as the area becomes more urbanized and developed and the total population continues to grow, each sector exerts pressure on the outward perimeter of its own sector. Generally each sector may be well defined through some geographical boundary or marker, such as a river, railroad track, major roadway, or a variety of other such identifiable features. Another feature that has developed as a consequence of such patterns of development is that with growth and new building occurring at the perimeter of such cities, the inner city core is left to be occupied by either the very poor or by no one at all. Most often the very poor tend to dominate the former city core areas which have been left by the more affluent classes for the new amenities of the suburban developments.

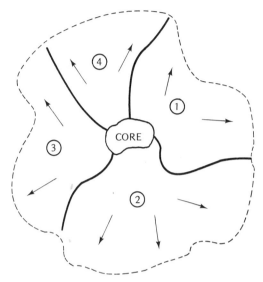

Figure 7-4 *Sector Patterns*

Although most cities do not easily lend themselves to the circle and wedges of the sector theory, there is strong evidence for the concept of a sector type of development pattern in many cities. Generally people do congregate in separate groups for working as well as for living in the domestic sense. Such grouping can be easily described in the form of many sectors of populations within a city, each exerting pressure in one major direction as that group or minicommunity grows in population.

The identification of such groups and their growth trends greatly aids in the understanding of the growth patterns of a community at large. For the most part, such tendency to congregate by income class is more a function of economics than of other factors. The maximum in terms of space and amenities, given a predefined income level, is essentially what each member of each group is seeking to obtain. The additional factors of social intercourse with others of a common education, cultural, or social level, commonly are secondary factors after the income and cost constraints have been accommodated.

HISTORICAL LAND USE PATTERNS

The majority of the land use theories have been based on the facts of history that resulted in the various patterns of development of the cities which became established over the past history. Primarily such patterns were a function of three major forces. First, the natural and man-made boundaries or barriers which shaped the cities from the outset. Things such as rivers, valleys, hills, fortifications for defense, and port facilities were the major factors in the old cities. The second major factor in the pattern of city growth was the transportation systems allocated to, in, and throughout such cities. The patterns and routes of canals, railroads, and roads were a major causative factor in the patterns of development which continued after such facilities were constructed.

The development of the automobile alone probably had more direct influence on the patterns of growth and development of the cities in the western half of the United States than any other single factor. The ability of energy resources to grow and accommodate large and spread-out populations was a key factor; but even these were allocated largely along the automobile roads that tended to precede them. Until the late twentieth century, man was very much a prisoner of his environment in terms of the land use patterns that developed. Geography, climate, and the advantages or disadvantages of nature had as much or more to say about the patterns of city development than the collective minds of the peoples concerned.

THE NEW STAGE OF LAND USE PATTERNS

In the late 1960s the American community, as well as others, seriously began to entertain the concept that man had entered a phase in history where the technology of mankind had reached the point that new cities and towns no longer had to conform to the past development patterns dictated by history and the dependence on the gifts or lack of gifts on the part of nature. Technology had reached a point where cities could be built from the very beginning virtually anywhere. Factors such as terrain, climate, and natural resources could be overcome through careful planning and the selective use of new technology.

After serious study and evaluation, several large real estate concerns attempted large-scale projects such as complete new towns. Although some of these so-called new towns were nothing more than large residential and "bedroom" communities, some were, in fact, heterogeneous communities from the very beginning. A few such as Reston, Virginia, and Irvine, California, were successful to some degree. But the mere scale of commitment, and the enormous variety of interrelated activities, resources, and economic and social/cultural interests, generally were far beyond the capabilities of any single firm—no matter how large—to assume.

The federal government was quickly involved in the financial aspects of such projects, and even then several were on the very edge of default. There is no doubt that a large factor in the timing of problems encountered by such developers was the sudden turndown in the economy of the nation at a time when those same firms were out of necessity highly leveraged in these projects; and the delay or slowdown in sales performance led to an inability to maintain the interest payments on the huge amounts of debt that such projects incurred. Although we now have the technology with which to overcome the parameters of city growth in the past, we still have a great deal to learn and understand about human beings and how they evaluate their personal best interests in terms of their tendency toward urbanized family living.

THE PRINCIPLE OF COMPARATIVE ADVANTAGE

In the field of international economics, the comparative cost analysis is presented as the classical case in support of trade between two countries. Figure 7-5 illustrates the example in a matrix form. If country (A) is able to produce 10 units of meat to every 5 units of grain, and the total sunken cost is $3,000, then, if it must produce both to survive, its total production will be 15 units at a unit cost of $200 each. Country (B) is in the exact opposite position with the same total output and the same unit cost of $200 for each unit. Now if it were possible for trade to begin between these two areas, then each area could produce that which it was most efficient—in terms of lower cost and higher output—at producing. Figure 7-6 illustrates the same two areas, but with the ability to trade between the two areas now established. As a result, each country will now specialize only in producing that which it can produce most efficiently. As a result, the total output of each country rises by one-third; and the unit cost for each item to all consumers of that item is reduced by one-fourth.

	MEAT	GRAIN	TOTAL	UNIT COST $= \frac{3000}{\text{T.O.}}$
"A"	10	5	15	200
"B"	5	10	15	200
	15	15	30	

Figure 7-5   *Closed Economy—without trade*

	MEAT	GRAIN	TOTAL	UNIT COST $= \frac{3000}{\text{T.O.}}$
"A"	20	ϕ	20	150
"B"	ϕ	20	20	150
	20	20	40	

Figure 7-6   *Open Economy—with trade*

If instead of two separate countries we substituted two geographical areas within the same city or region, which would also have very few or no impediments to trade and exchange between them, it becomes quite clear why certain areas within a region quickly become dominated by one type of industry or one predominant type of land use. Those sites with the greatest number of advantages will tend to attract uses that are more intense and specialized in their requirements.

Highly intensive land uses such as office buildings, home offices, high-rise buildings of a variety of types, will tend to locate at sites with the greatest number of advantages because their use allows the greatest returns with which to bid for such sites. The less intensive land uses do not carry as great returns associated with the land location, and therefore they are precluded from bidding as high in the free market for such sites. Similarly the requirements for residential land uses are not as stringent as those for specialized office structures, and residential will generally be less inclined to bid as high for such specific locations. Therefore those sites which are able to produce the specific service at the lowest cost will tend to produce such services almost exclusively. Such comparative cost figures represent costs as well as total output, for total output will frequently reduce the per unit cost if such total is quite large. It can then be seen why communities often enter into competitive advertising and bidding contests in their attempts to attract new industry and commerce to an area. Incentives such as investment credits, free or very low-cost buildings and structures built to the company's specifications, and very often a moratorium on local property and business taxes, have a real impact on the real cost of doing business in one area versus another.

CONTINUOUS SITE COMPETITION

This brings us immediately to our next chapter that is very closely related to the principle of comparative advantage. The concept of continuous site competition is based on the idea that every available site in a given real estate market is competing with every other site for every type of use to which the land may be put. Each landowner would perhaps like it quite well if instead of his home, someone was willing to buy his property and erect a 40-story building on that side. In such a case, the landowner would most probably realize a very large profit from the sale. The reason that generally this is not the case is through the concept of continuous site competition. Every other piece of property in that community is also competing for that same office building. As a result, of all the possible sites in the community competing for such use, the site with the greatest total advantage will tend to attract the highest and most intensive use.

PROFILE OF PROPORTIONALITY

As a result of the principle of continuous site competition, most cities and towns develop a profile in cross section that shows a vigorous use of land at the city center, and then gradually decreasing land use intensity as one moves from the city center out toward the perimeters of the city. If one carried such a cross section completely out of the city, it progresses from high-rise structures at the very center out to farmland and eventually even further out to vacant land even unsuitable for intense agriculture. Figure 7-7 illustrates this proportionality of a city cross section.

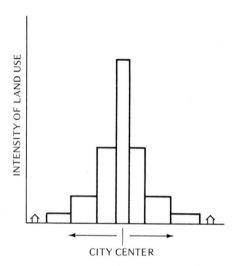

Figure 7-7   *Principle of Proportionality*

At the very center of town would be the high-rise buildings. The next level of land use could be the several-story retail and business firms, but definitely less intense than at the very center. The next land use would tend to be the general retail stores and service firms, which are seldom more than two to four stories high. As one continues to move out from the center, the so-called commercial strip could be the next most intensive land use. These might be single-level retail and service outlets in the suburbs and along the radial corridors. This would also tend to contain the multifamily residential units of most areas.

Finally might come the single-family detached housing of the community.

Beyond the residential area would lie the small farms and country homes, the truck farms, leading to the full-fledged farming areas, and then to the open land areas of no cultivation. Such open areas may be forested, or in open grasslands or rangelands used for cattle grazing. Such areas may also be in the form of parks, recreational areas, and national forests. The major point is that at the far outer limits of urbanization there occurs a very low level of intensity in terms of the uses to which the land areas are assigned.

THE CONCEPT OF HIGHEST AND BEST USE

There is probably no single concept more widely accepted and used in the determination of the uses to which land within urban areas is put than the concept of the highest and best use. No matter what the social arguments to the contrary may be, highest and best use has generally been used to describe that use to which real property is put and which yields the highest economic return associated with that location to the owners of the land itself. The concept is an economic one and is therefore measured according to the yardstick available to the economist. The measurement of advantages or disadvantages in the economic sphere is the monetary scale; that is the results are translated into dollar costs and profits. So long as the motives of the principle involved are confined to the economic sphere, then such a measurement tool is accurate.

The primary disadvantage of the economic criteria, however, is the lack of an effective measurement of a social good. The costs of social goods are well identified through economic analysis, but the gains or benefits of such social goods are not and should not be measured in terms of dollars and cents. So long as we confine our analysis to the lowest cost three-bedroom home, we can make an analysis of a rather dependable nature on such houses at various points throughout a city. But what does one do when comparing houses for families against more green spaces, or more lakes and rivers to swim in, or clean air to breathe?

Individuals can make a fairly rational judgment between alternative costs versus the benefits of living in one location or another. Where is there a measurement that is uniformly accepted for the ascertainment of the benefits of clean water for swimming, or more open space? The tools of economics are not meant and are not suitable for the measurement of the benefits to be derived from the social goods. Agreeing with and accepting the limitations of the tools of economics, we must also accept their appropriateness for the measurement of the costs of social goods, and leave to the world of personal value judgment the collective conclusion as to the worth of the benefits to be derived from such costly investments in social necessities and amenities.

One final comment on the concept of the highest and best use of any property: The highest and best use is an economic concept, and therefore defined in the marketplace through the interplay of economic alternatives and forces. Highest and best use may be restricted by various public and semipublic agencies, but it is not defined by them. Highest and best use is not a divine statement, but rather the calculated conclusion of the individuals in the marketplace assuming risks and making decisions. More on this point will follow in the next chapter.

SELECTED READINGS

Chermayeff, Serge, and Tzonis. *Alexander Shape of Community*. Baltimore: Penguin Books, 1971.

Ewald, William R. *Environment for Man*. Bloomington, Ind.: Indiana University Press, 1967.

Finkler, Earl, and David L. Peterson. *Nongrowth Planning Strategies*. New York: Praeger Publishers, 1974.

Fuller, R. Buckminster. *Utopia or Oblivion*. New York: Bantam Books, 1969.

Goodman, Paul, and Percival Goodman. *Communities*. New York: Vintage Books, 1960.

Hoyt, Homer, Arthur M. Weimer, and George F. Bloom. *Real Estate*. 6th ed. Chicago, Ill.: The Ronald Press, 1972.

More, Thomas. *Utopia*. Baltimore: Penguin Books, 1965.

Park, Robert E. et al. *The City*. Chicago: University of Chicago Press, 1967.

CHAPTER EIGHT

PLANNING AND CONTROL OF LAND USE

Controls over the uses to which land may be put are not evenly distributed throughout the citizenry. There are some groups and agents that have a great deal of control over the way in which real property in their region or under their influence may be used. On the other hand, for the majority of individuals depending on where the land they own or are concerned about is located, for the most part they have or exercise very little influence over the land use decision area which is so important in our daily lives.

PRIVATE CONTROLS

The individual owner of real property may use his or her property in any way desired, within the parameters of the legal constraints in the area or community within which such land area is located. For the owner of land in fee-simple ownership, such an owner has nearly complete authority to use such land, and to make improvements on such land area as his or her personal tastes and wishes dictate. As such, the control over the use of the land in the basic sense lies directly within the confines of the owner of that property.

There are many instances, however, in which a previous owner has made stipulations about the use of certain properties, and which were expressed at the time of sale by that previous owner. Generally such restrictions have been grouped under the class known as covenants, conditions, and restrictions.

COVENANTS, CONDITIONS, AND RESTRICTIONS (CC&Rs)

Covenants, conditions, and restrictions are actually the same type of control over land use; the primary difference is the remedy for a failure to live and operate by the restrictions over land use so expressed. There are, however, three requirements for such CC&Rs to be enforceable. These requirements are:

1. Restrictions must be in writing. Oral agreements between buyer and seller are not valid or enforceable in a court of law. Restrictions must also be recorded in a deed with each property so affected by such restrictions.
2. Restrictions must be mandatory by each landowner. If such restrictions are optional, they then are not considered restrictions and are therefore no longer enforceable.
3. Finally, restrictions must concern and touch the land itself and the use to which it is put. Restrictions related to race or ethnic or religious character of the buyer, now or in the future, do not touch or concern the land. Rather such restrictions affect the people on the land, and therefore have been held to be unenforceable and invalid.

The primary difference between a condition, a restriction, and a covenant is the remedy available for the violation of such restrictions. In a simple deed *restriction* the grantor, or adjacent property owners affected by such restriction, may seek enforcement of such a deed restriction in court. The remedy of the court is to issue an injunction against the violator of the deed restriction. Continued violation would result in the party being held in contempt of court and going to prison.

In a *covenant*, the restriction and its agreement is the basis of a binding contract between the grantor (seller) and the grantee (buyer). If the grantee violates the restriction, the grantor may sue the grantee in a court of law for breach of contract. It is exactly the same as a restriction, except that the remedy is money damages awarded for a breach of contract rather than an injunction issued by the court.

The *condition* is probably the strongest of the three classes of private restrictions. Although it is merely a restriction with a different remedy for violation, that remedy makes covenants quite powerful. If the one subject to a covenant violates such a covenant, there is a reverter clause in the deed which provides that in open violation of such a covenant the title to the land reverts back to the grantor of the deed originally. Where a violation of a condition would result in the total loss of all interest in the subject property, there is a very powerful inclination on the part of the grantee to live by the letter of such conditions.

In recent years, in the United States there has been a growing number of planned communities which in many cases attempted to carry a theme of mood throughout such a development. The growth in condominium types of developments has also led to the growing use and importance of things such as covenants, conditions, and restrictions. It is through these instruments that the developers of such communities can maintain the effect and atmosphere in the design—and also through the assurance such restrictions give the potential home buyer, that his or her investment will be well maintained—that the developer is able to attract a higher price for his product than perhaps would be the case if such restrictions as to use were not included.

Finally, there tend to be a great number of common facilities in such developments, to be used by all owners in the community. The CC&Rs included in the deed of every unit provide for the manner in which the facilities are to be maintained and managed. Also set out is the manner in which the Homeowners Association, which is responsible for such management of common areas, is to be organized and the rights of each member. The range of subjects included in such CC&Rs as in a condominium project may cover pets, number and age of guests, length of stay, children and grandchildren, patio areas and what may be exposed in such areas, security, painting, landscaping, architecture of modifications, and a multitude of areas which virtually cover every aspect of real property ownership. The intent is to protect and insure the overall worth of the development, and the peace and tranquility of the individuals owning property in such a development.

One thought of a large pair of Saint Bernard dogs in a downtown 20-story luxury condominium project quickly clarifies the motivation on the part of the developer of such a project to include a set of CC&Rs for the peace of mind and security of the investment on the part of the eventual owners of such units. In the tract housing developments, things such as no front fences, prohibitions against motor homes and campers and trailers seen from the front street, trees above certain height obstructing the view of the nearby homeowners, are but a few of the types of restrictions included in the list of CC&Rs that every homeowner of such a tract receives.

PUBLIC CONTROLS OVER LAND USE

ZONING

Probably the single most obvious way in which the public sector exercises direct control over the land use patterns of a community is through what are known as zoning codes. These codes are municipal codes, passed and written by the local citizenry and they tend to vary a great deal from one community to another. Unincorporated areas also have zoning codes, but those codes are enacted by the county administrative body.

Often there is a misconception on the part of people as to where such zoning originated. Zoning, as we know it in the United States, is very much an American concept. The first zoning commissions were founded in the early 1920s; and it was not until the Supreme Court of the United States endorsed such zoning in 1926, that it became an accepted method for controlling and coordinating the land use within municipal areas. Nearly all zoning codes and laws on the local levels originated during the early 1930s as a direct result of the Supreme Court's decision. So we have less than 50 years' experience in the implementation and enforcement of the zoning concept of regulating land use and growth patterns on the local level.

The basis of such zoning powers on the part of municipalities lies in the police power of the constitution given to the individual states. Since the states are responsible for the general health and safety of the population, they are able to regulate the use and composition of communities for the benefit of an entire community. Such police power on the part of the state is given to the local administration as the first line of implementation. The rationale behind zoning ordinances has been that by separating the uses of property and confining certain uses to certain areas, then fire and police protection could be more easily maintained.

It is significant, however, that not all communities have zoning laws and zoning codes for their community. The most notable exception to the widespread use of zoning commissions and codes is probably the city of Houston, Texas. The primary method of land use control in that city is through the use of deed restrictions imposed by individual landowners and being well founded in terms of overall impact on the community. Many smaller communities have no zoning ordinances, and yet are able to maintain a well coordinated use of land areas.

REGIONAL PLANNING AGENCIES

As a result of the inability of several local municipal jurisdictions to effectively control the land use patterns and to coordinate the land use within a regional context, of which all municipalities were a part, the federal government, through the Department of Housing and Urban Development, began to encourage the formation of regional planning agencies. Although the federal government does not have jurisdiction over local areas within individual states so far as land use was concerned, through requiring such a regional polling agency to review and evaluate applications by such local governments for federal funds, the federal government wielded a very big stick indeed.

The federal government effectively froze all federal support for individual projects until all such regions could assemble and together form some regional planning body. It was not very long until such agencies were actually formed, and they had a general land use plan for the region drawn and on file with that agency for inspection by the representatives of the federal programs involved. It was in recognition that we are essentially members of economic areas, and that what one town does in terms of zoning and land use regulations will surely affect its neighbors. But it should also be recognized that the addition of another layer of bureaucracy in the decision-making process tends to result in additional time-lags and an increase in the costs of the projects involved.

LIMITATIONS OF ZONING

The emphasis of zoning regulations is on the future development and changes contemplated in the land use patterns of a community. As of the effective date of the zoning code or changes in it, all improvements on the area of land concerned are not touched by such new zoning restrictions. All present structures and uses to which such structures are put are immune from the new requirements of the municipal zoning laws. All new buildings and improvements must conform to the zoning regulations in effect at the time they are begun; but once construction has begun on land areas covered by a new ordinance, such improvements are subject only to that law in effect prior to construction.

Structures which do not conform to the new zoning code are also allowed to remain, provided they had begun prior to the new regulations. Zoning has no control over the nonconforming uses to which it is put within the subject area. The provisions of such zoning regulations does not provide for any mechanism by which to correct such nonconforming uses. In fact the courts have held that retroactive zoning, that zoning which would correct nonconforming uses, is inherently unconstitutional.

Finally, zoning affects the use to which real property within its jurisdiction may be put; but it does not affect the architectural style or design features of the improvements made on such land. So long as the use to which the land and improvements are put is authorized under the zoning code, the zoning authorities are totally without any further control over such improvements.

SPECIAL REDEVELOPMENT AGENCIES

In the late 1960s and early 1970s the federal, state, and local governments began to be very concerned with the trend toward degeneration of the downtown cores of many of our major cities. There were special pieces of legislation that provided needed funds for the redevelopment of those areas at lower cost and with partial support from the federal government. In such cases, an area would be defined for redevelopment. Once the area was defined, a formal and detailed plan for its restoration was developed.

For the city involved, the major way in which such programs worked financially was to freeze the tax base at its present level; then through general revenue bonds providing the funding, the structures within the area would be demolished or restored as was most feasible. The building and restoration was done through private landowners, but according to the architectural guidelines set down in the redevelopment plan.

Through the incentive of low-cost financing and long loan periods, the private investors and owners were persuaded to make the restoration or the rebuilding according to the outlined overall architectural theme. In cases in which the owners did not wish to or were not capable of restoring or building according to architectural theme, the agency would condemn the property and buy it; and then restore or build according to the plan and sell the structure on completion. In either case, the redevelopment agency would have affective control over the architectural style of the improvements in that area. Such control would have been totally impossible under the normal zoning and planning powers.

BUILDING CODES

Most municipalities and counties for unincorporated areas have a set of building codes which are very specific in terms of the material requirements for structures built on subject land within such jurisdiction. The codes may be bound separately, each dealing with a specific area of concern. For example, many areas have a separate building code, a separate electrical code, and a separate plumbing code. Each code spells out exactly what types of materials, angle, stresses, and sizes must be used for every area covered by these codes.

Building codes will state the size of timbers for bearing and nonbearing walls; the type and size of Sheetrock or plaster to be put on the structure; the minimum size of window and door headers; and a multitude of other very specific areas each of which requires inspection at various stages during construction. The plumbing code will state the size and angles of water and drain piping to be employed; and the angles and diameters of various venting pipes to be installed, as well as the location of such plumbing lines in relation to the other structures within the project. And plumbing also is subject to required tests of security of the water, drain, and gas lines. The electrical inspections and code must specify the size of wiring, where circuits are to be accessible, what the maximum circuits on a line are, as well as the total service input requirement to a building.

Furthermore, these building codes also apply to older structures already in place. In most instances, new code requirements will be applied only to substantial repairs, expansion, or replacement of the items covered below. However, in some municipalities the buildings must be brought up to any new code requirements prior to being sold or transferred. Although preexisting uses are exempt from new zoning regulations covering the use of real property, the building codes of that same jurisdiction are also applied to older structures.

HEALTH AND SAFETY REGULATIONS

The departments of public health and safety of the various municipalities throughout the country are responsible for the enforcement of basic laws related to sanitary conditions, maintenance and repair, water and heating, and the various fire and safety codes. These regulations are meant to help keep communities free from epidemics of disease and filth, and also to protect the general population from unnecessary losses due to fire, flood, or other major threats. As a consequence, there have developed a set of laws regulating the facilities within a structure as well as the state and condition of the structure itself. The requirements of fire escapes of certain types and sizes, depending on a building and its use; the requirement of hand railing on all stairwells wider than a certain width; and a variety of other such specific regulations are examples of the health and safety codes that all structures within certain jurisdictions must meet.

Many times the competing goals of market attractiveness and public safety meet head on. An example would be the requirement of internal overhead sprinkler systems on all holdings higher than three floors, and at the same time an attempt to refurbish very old masonry buildings of the Victorian style which were totally impractical and economically unfeasible to plumb for such sprinkling systems.

PUBLIC OWNERSHIP OF LAND

FEDERAL GOVERNMENT

According to the General Services Administration, the federal government owns nearly 500,000 buildings in 50 states and territories. That is nearly 50,000 buildings for each state! In addition to improvements, the federal government owns and controls a tremendous amount of the total land area in the country. The federal government of the United States owns nearly one-half of the total land in the entire state of California, and more than three-quarters of the land in our largest state, Alaska. The majority of the land owned by the federal government is located west of the Mississippi River, therefore most western states will tend to have control over slightly more or less than the example of California. In general, the Eastern states have perhaps more buildings but less land area owned by the federal branch of government.

Although the bureaus of the federal government attempt to cooperate with the desires and wishes of the local citizens insofar as the location and construction of federal facilities is concerned, communication is at best haphazard. As a result, most often the federal government and its agencies build and locate improvements pretty well where they deem them appropriate.

When the desires of the local citizens for a post office facility, or for a military outpost, or for a government facility of any type run against the budget constraints of the bureau or agency responsible, the bureau or agency nearly always prevails. Similarly the national defense or security of the nation takes precedence over the desires of a local group of citizens opposed to the location of a government facility in their community.

The location of government installations such as prisons, reform schools, supply depots, military bases, hospitals, and many other types of facilities can affect the pattern of development and land use in a local area to a very significant degree. Not only are prisons not found in stable upper-income or middle-class residential areas, but branch post offices are. Generally the same would be true for service and military establishments not being located in predominantly residential areas. Additionally, depending on the type of facility built, there is a spillover impact on the servicing sector of the local economy, and the increased burdens associated with traffic of vehicles in and out of a military facility, and the provisions for the transport of people in and out of those same facilities.

The whole area of increased pressure on the school and hospital facilities of an area are easily seen. What is not seen at first is the commitment to capital investments in increased sewer and water treatment facilities, increased power demands for the homes and families of the workers of such federal facilities, as well as the increased demand for those same facilities on the part of the facility itself.

The opposite picture is seldom studied with much earnest interest prior to such being the case. What is the community to be left with if such facility is cut back or entirely phased out? What type of burden, in the form of day-to-day activities as well as the long-term financing of improved roads and other public services, is required by the people of such a facility? Additionally, in the event of such a cutback or reduction of the activity of such a facility, what public services are available for the restraining and support during the relocation process? The complexities and political aspects of the decision-making processes, involving the inventory and state of affairs with respect to the buildings and land holdings of the federal government, are such that they are seldom completely understood by the communities involved, and, furthermore, rarely ever completely accommodated.

STATE GOVERNMENTS

The individual states are also very large land owners, including such things as hospitals, universities, parks, and recreational areas. As with the federal government, there are also vast holdings of capital improvements on the part of the states. Each state has a vast amount of land taken up in roads and state highways. As earlier discussed, the location of roads and highways has a very large impact on the patterns of growth and development of an area; and the condition of such roads also has a great deal to do with the ability of such routes to support the economic activities of the area or region that depend on them.

With reference to educational facilities, universities are a major factor in the type and patterns of development which occur in a region or area. Large universities such as most state universities often include a great deal of research. Research such as in the areas of medicine and high technology most often attracts a growing light-manufacturing industry that markets and develops such results from the university close by. Examples would include the Boston area, the lower San Francisco Bay near Stanford University, and many others of similar characteristics.

The location and commitment on the part of state governments to such university systems and facilities actually constitutes a basic industry segment of a local economy, and many nonbasic industries generally grow very rapidly as such universities become established and grow. A university with a student body of over 20,000 students comes much closer to becoming another city with a total population that includes the service sector of at least twice that many.

GOVERNMENT AGENCIES

In the 1970s there has been a growing trend toward more specific government agencies at virtually all levels that are assigned the responsibility for specific areas of development and the consequences of such growth and development. Perhaps an example would illustrate more clearly what those agencies include.

Assume for a moment that the area of study includes several hundred acres in an estuary area on the Pacific Coast and a short distance from an international boundary. Furthermore, there also happens to be a river running into the estuary, and also there is a military air base within a short distance. The following agencies are responsible for one or more aspects of the subject area: The Coastal Commission, the National Park Service, the U.S. Customs, the Defense Department, the Environmental Protection Agency, the State Department, the Commission on Flood Control, the Army Corps of Engineers, and a variety of local agencies and commissions. If a residential project were being contemplated, the long list would also include the Department of Housing and Urban Development, as well as the state Real Estate Commission.

All these government agencies have the power to veto a project, but not one of them has the total authority to approve a project. It takes unanimous approval of all the agencies to start a project, and only one dissenting agency can terminate the proposal. These agencies have enormous negative power and rarely exert any amount of positive influence over projects. That is not their function; and therefore the result is such a mirage of bureaus that these agencies affect nearly every project and every citizen in the country. In such a way, these agencies, at all levels of government, have a very real impact and influence on the land use patterns and the development that occurs in our contemporary society.

ECONOMIC IMPACT OF CONTROLS

To a very large extent, the success or failure of a project to make it through the bureaucratic maze is dependent as much on luck and political happenstance as on the economic forces entailed in the project. As such, the results of the interaction between supply and demand in the marketplace are quite blurred by the levels of bureaucracy involved. Whenever an increasing numbers of things are placed between the buyer and the seller in the marketplace, the results are in the form of decisions relating to price of product in exchange and the ultimate use or returns associated with that transaction are very much divorced from the economic forces that brought the buyer and seller together in the first place.

As such, the displacement of economic forces in the allocation process of goods and services by social and political forces is neither good nor bad. The major area of complaint for the student of such processes is the loss of one useful form of analysis and measurement, and the gaining of a form of analysis more abstract and loose in definition of terms, and totally lacking in acceptable units of measure. Social consequences are impossible to measure in a uniform manner, and virtually excluded from comparison with one another. Finally, such blurring of the market forces also tends to lead to great fluctuation as a result of the shifting political tide to which government action is subject.

Another consequence of the increase in the time-lags, and the increase in risk associated with winning the final approval of a proposed project, is that not all projects make it through the approval maze. Also a very good number of proposed projects are withdrawn before they ever enter the elimination process. The net result is that fewer projects and fewer units are built. When the amount supplied is decreased due to the inability of the suppliers to assume the liability of the increased time-lags and the decrease in the probability of approval the first time through, the consequence in terms of the marketplace is a rise in the price of the product or service. Figure 8-1 illustrates this consequence.

When the amount supplied in the marketplace drops from Q_1 to Q_2, the result is a rise in the price of a product or service from the former equilibrium price of P_1 to P_2. The drop in production of housing units in the United States from a level of about 2 million units per year from 1971 through 1974, to barely 1 million units in 1975, must be at least partially attributable to the increased risks and costs involved in the approval process.

The next major area of consequence in terms of the approval and control aspects is the tendency of that approval process to raise costs, and therefore raise the ultimate price of the product or service. Whenever the time involved in the decision-making process and in the projection process is increased it results in a

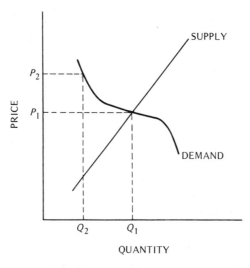

Figure 8-1   *Effects of Controls on Supply*

very direct and immediate increase in the costs of the project. Time is one of the most expensive of all items in any project, and time cannot be recovered or slowed down.

In nearly every real estate project the role of financing and leveraged money is a very important one. Whenever money is borrowed, the rent on such money is a function of time. Although perhaps unfair, it has been my experience that most bureaucrats have a total misconception of time. Time is not free; it is very, very expensive. Delays in time are quickly reflected in a dramatic rise in costs of completion, and in the prices when the finished product will be offered for sale. The extension of the gestation period of a real estate development project to well over two years from the beginning of the investment by the owner to the first shovel of dirt, has a prodigious impact on the market performance of the real estate industry and the crisis in which the current market finds itself. With an average sale price of well over $40,000 nearly three-fourths of the entire population of our country are priced out of the market for decent housing.

Eventually the control maze creates a situation where the only market that can effectively remain being served is the rather well-to-do income groups. The high-priced product tends to be in a less elastic area of the demand function for real estate, and therefore can tolerate a shift upward in the price. There are two major problems with such emphasis on the part of the suppliers of real estate. First, more than three-fourths of the market is no longer being served by the market forces, but rather three-fourths of the market is being disserved by the market. The market will not turn to the levels of control and approval, but rather to the real estate market itself to register complaints.

Second, the high-priced market is a very thin market. That is, although relatively inelastic, the market of high-priced exclusive residential real estate is a small market in terms of the total number of units which that market is able to absorb. The result is that such a market, particularly on a local level, is very quickly overbuilt. When that market is overbuilt, there are virtually no customers left at all who can absorb such units at anywhere near the costs of constructing them. The luxury condominium market in many local areas was the scene of much overbuilding, and the result was that a great number of builders and financial institutions lost a great deal of money.

There are very real and significant costs associated with government approval processes involving real estate. Such costs and their impact should be known and understood in order for the suppliers as well as the ultimate customers in the real estate sector to meet and adjust to the demands of the nation's real estate needs.

SELECTED READINGS

Anderson, Ronald A., and Walter A. Kumpf. *Business Law.* 6th ed. Cincinnati: South-Western Publishing Co., 1975.

Bosselman, Fred, and David Callies. *The Quiet Revolution in Land Use Control for the Council on Environmental Quality.* Washington, D.C.: U.S. Government Printing Office, 1971.

Kratovil, Robert. *Real Estate Law.* 6th ed. Englewood Cliffs, N.J.: Prentice-Hall, Inc., 1974.

Makielski, S. J., Jr. *The Politics of Zoning.* New York: Columbia University Press, 1966.

Moynihan, Daniel P. *Toward a National Urban Policy*. New York: Basic Books, Inc., 1970.

Perloff, Harvey S. *The Future of the United States Government*. New York: George Braziller, Inc., for: The American Academy of Arts and Sciences, 1971.

PART FIVE

INSTITUTIONAL INFLUENCES

We now turn our attention to the unique role played by the various institutional factors insofar as the land use patterns of urbanized areas are determined and shaped. The first major sector of institutional influence is, of course, the role of the federal, state, and local government. It is a very large role in terms of the outright ownership of large land areas, and the control and influence of the remaining privately held land areas through a variety of agencies and powers at all levels. Such factors are vitally important in terms of the land use patterns and trends in urbanization processes. Problems as well as solutions lie at the doorstep of many governmental bodies.

The second major institutional influence is the wide range of private institutions that control great sectors of real property, or the elements that great land areas rely on for supportive services. Elements such as transportation, banking, finance, lending, building, and many other areas of the private sector are very important in the roles they play with regard to the use and improvements of real property. Factors such as employment and development are critical to virtually every major urban area of nearly any size.

CHAPTER NINE

THE ROLE OF GOVERNMENT

ECONOMIC PHILOSOPHY

From the Middle Ages onward, the merchant class has progressively gained more power and influence primarily through its ability to accumulate vast sums of capital through trade and commerce. The real freedom of the middle class and merchants from the constraints of the monarchy and/or the Church was brought about by the Industrial Revolution. The advantages that constituted the industrialization process were so great, the power of the industrialists grew to be nearly equal to that of the ruling class. The implicit assumption behind such freedom was that the growth of the industrial sector and its owners would invariably help the growth of the nations concerned.

Under the doctrine of capitalism each individual was assumed to operate in the marketplace in such a way as to advance his or her own self-interest. This tenet has been called the profit maximization assumption. Under the laissez-faire form of capitalism, which literally means hands off, the individual owners of capital resources were free to perform any way they saw fit in the marketplace to advance their own position. The profit motive was the only motive or result accepted in the economic system of the time, and was thought to be the best for the individuals involved and the nation as a whole.

It was not until the turn of the century in the United States that the entire country began to seriously discern the difference between social and economic goods. (Some of the social impact of such unbridled profits maximization was simply too gross and too harmful to be tolerated on the part of the nation and its people.)Furthermore, the power that began to be concentrated in the hands of a few very successful industrialists soon led to corruption within the political system itself. (As a result of such consequences, the government began to assert itself as the overall power force in the country and burdened with the responsibility of protecting the rights and welfare of all citizens.)At this time many of the very large and powerful industrial trusts were broken up, and competition was partially reestablished as the positive force in the market to assure that both buyers and sellers of goods and services would be well and fairly treated in the marketplace.

Within 50 years' time there developed a growing involvement on the part of state and federal governments to the point in the current period where government of one form or another is directly involved in nearly every aspect of every business. Such a form of economic philosophy may well be called a controlled form of capitalism.

The role of the profit motive is still central to the allocation process of goods and services. The alternative to individual decision-making in the marketplace—in relation to the quality and price of a product or service—is some form of centralized policy decision-making. It is my opinion that the collective intelligence in government policy commissions is certainly no more, and perhaps less, than the ability of individuals to make their personal decisions in relation to importance of goods or services in terms of their personal wealth. The growing elements of capitalism even in dogmatic nations, such as the USSR, would seem to verify the inherent advantages of a decentralized method for the allocation of goods and services.

MONETARY POLICY

The management and control of the supply of capital or money in a country is called the monetary policy of that nation. In the United States, such policy is the responsibility of the Federal Reserve System. The Federal Reserve System is the central banking system of the United States. There are twelve Federal Reserve banks in the Federal Reserve System, one for each of the twelve districts. As the board of governors of the Federal Reserve System meet, the need on the part of the economy for more or less money in the system is discussed, and decisions are made on a weekly basis as to the level of interest rates and the inflationary pressures are measured against the level of the economic activity of the nation.

In a depressed state of economic activity, the expansion of the money supply may be indicated so as to lower the cost of borrowing to the major business sector. In a highly inflationary period the need may be to cool the economy down a bit through reducing the supply of money, and thus raising the cost of borrowed capital. The monetary policy on the part of the treasury and Federal Reserve System with reference to interest rates and the level of inflationary pressures acceptable for the health of the economy are the primary areas of monetary policy.

THE RESERVE REQUIREMENT

The first tool of controlling the money supply is the requirement of maintaining a certain percentage of total deposits on hand to meet the cash needs of withdrawals. Such a percentage level of reserves to deposits is called the reserve requirement. Funds in excess of the reserves can be lent out in the form of business loans and personal loans. The reserves cannot be lent out, and therefore, in a general way, do not reflect income generating assets.

Changes in the reserve requirement very directly and immediately affect the level of loanable funds in the member banks. If for every $100.00 a bank had to retain 15 percent as a reserve, then they would have $85.00 to loan out. If that reserve requirement were raised to 20 percent, then that same bank would find itself with only $80.00 to lend out to its customers. When such figures are in hundreds of millions of dollars, the changes are indeed very significant.

The price in the form of interest for loanable funds would likewise be affected very directly and very quickly. The interest rate would tend to rise sharply when the amount of loanable funds was reduced through increasing the reserve requirement. Assuming that the demand for funds remained unchanged, the interest rate would fall rapidly when the reserve requirement was lowered and released more loanable funds into the financial system.

THE OPEN MARKET OPERATIONS

Because the reserve requirement is rather cumbersome to change on a weekly or monthly basis to meet the weekly changes in the economic activities of the commercial sector of our economy, the Federal Reserve System tends to rely much more on the operations of the Open Market Committee of the Federal Reserve System for the adjustments of a seasonal or weekly nature needed to accommodate the economic fluctuations of our very complex and dynamic economic system. The Open Market Committee is composed of seven members of the Board of Governors of the Federal Reserve System, with the chairman of the System always in attendance.

At the weekly meetings of their committee, the decision to buy and sell Treasury bills and other securities of the federal government is made in terms of amounts and the terms of such securities. The Open Market Committee of the Federal Reserve System meets every Tuesday of each week in the upper floors of the New York City Federal Reserve Bank. The decisions of the committee are executed on the very next day, and become public later that week. The discussions of the members of the committee, in terms of their intentions in acting the way they did, are not public for 30 days in order to prevent individuals from taking advantage of the system and negating what the Federal Reserve System is attempting to accomplish.

The Open Market Committee actually buys and sells securities of the federal government to member banks and associations. When the net difference between the number bought and number sold is an amount of notes or securities sold, there is a decrease in the money supply in the member banks. The Federal Reserve Bank will give the note or security in exchange for an amount of currency or account transfer from the member bank to the Federal Reserve Bank. When the Federal Reserve System is a net buyer of securities, the accounts of member banks are increased and the notes and securities held by the Federal Reserve System also increases. The net impact is that the money supply is increased when the Federal Reserve System is a net buyer of securities.

The impact of such actions on the part of the Federal Reserve System is to increase or decrease the supply or amount of money in the commercial banking system. When such supplies are increased, the interest rates tend to go down. When the supply of money goes down, the interest rates tend to rise. Capital to the business community, including the real estate community, is much like the blood in the body of a human being. We need blood to exist and survive, and blood must also keep in circulation. So it is with money or capital in the business community. The economy must have sufficient capital to conduct its activities, and the capital must be in such a form as to be steadily invested in production and the activity of business and personal transactions.

When funds are withdrawn from the economic system they filter through the system to reduce the funds, which are then available for business expansion and growth and the entire system of financing purchases by businesses and individuals has less capital with which to work. As the amount of capital is reduced, the priority for the use of existing money is given to immediate needs rather than additions to capital assets. Real estate, being a capital item, generally finds itself one of the first areas to suffer from loss of capital in times of a reduction in the supply of money in the economy.

FISCAL POLICY

The fiscal policy of a nation concentrates on the revenue and expenditure pattern of the federal government. It is not primarily concerned with the money supply or its fluctuations. Principally the areas of concern are the federal budget and whether or not such a budget is balanced or has a net deficit or a net surplus. A surplus in the federal budget means that the federal government and its agents will take in more money than they will be spending. The impact is a slight drain of funds from the economy. A budget surplus is considered to be a slightly anti-inflationary action because it tends to slow down the economy by taking funds out of the mainstream of business and consumer finance. These funds are then generally used either as an available revenue source for the following year, or to reduce the amount of debt owed by the federal government.

When the fiscal plan of the federal government provides for a deficit, it means that the federal government is spending more funds than it is taking in in the form of taxes and other revenue sources. The impact of such an action on the part of the federal government is primarily twofold. First, by spending more than it takes in, the federal government stimulates the economy through the hiring and business generated by its federal contracts and employment policies. For the most part, this results in a stimulus to inflation if such action occurs during a period when the economy is not substantially depressed.

The second major impact of a budget deficit on the part of the federal government is that it must finance overdrawn accounts through debt. When the government incurs debt, it sells securities—such as bonds—to the citizens of the country. In return for the bonds, the citizens give their savings or cash reserves. The major problem of this action on the part of the government is that the monies come out of the system which has a critical need for capital. When the federal government borrows money, it does so at a lower rate and usually in larger amounts than is done by private borrowers. The result is that the private sector is short of funds, at least to some degree. Such a shortage of funds most often results in a slowdown of growth and capital expansion, and a slight tendency to become even more reliant on the federal government sector for growth and economic activity.

When the federal government overdraws its account, it is much the same as when an individual overdraws his or her checking account. In the case of the individual, overdrawn checks must be immediately covered; otherwise they will not be

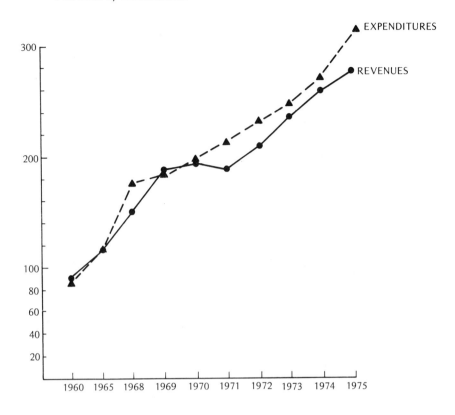

	REVENUE	EXPENDITURES	DIFFERENCE
1975	278,800,000,000	313,400,000,000	(34,600,000,000)
1974	264,900,000,000	268,400,000,000	(3,500,000,000)
1973	232,200,000,000	246,500,000,000	(14,300,000,000)
1972	208,600,000,000	231,900,000,000	(23,300,000,000)
1971	188,400,000,000	211,400,000,000	(23,000,000,000)
1970	193,700,000,000	196,600,000,000	(2,900,000,000)
1969	187,800,000,000	184,500,000,000	3,300,000,000
1968	153,700,000,000	178,800,000,000	(25,100,000,000)
1965	116,800,000,000	118,400,000,000	(1,600,000,000)
1960	92,500,000,000	92,200,000,000	300,000,000

Figure 9-1 *Fiscal Policy of Federal Government Receipts vs Expenditures (in billions of dollars).*

Source: U.S. Bureau of the Census, *Statistical Abstract of the United States,* 1975 (96th ed.). Washington, D.C., 1975, p. 225.

honored for payment. The adjustment on the part of the individual is immediate, and the income for such overdraws comes out of the current month's income. This adjustment also means that the spending and income patterns of the individual must be adjusted for the following month. In the case of the federal government, however, as is very often the case, such adjustment to balance accounts does not tend to take place at all. In fact, the deficit patterns from the middle 1960s and up to the present time seem to point in the direction of a continuing increase in such overdrawing regardless of the economic conditions of the time.

The impact of federal monetary and fiscal policy, with reference to the patterns and trends of urbanization, are significant and far-reaching. In a direct way, such actions on the part of the federal government affect the rate of economic growth and productivity directly through control of the supply and cost of capital needed for the operation and expansion of business activities. Second, the patterns of expenditure on the part of the federal government have a great impact on the selected areas affected.

Expenditures on the part of the federal government in such areas as mass transit and new energy technology have a very large impact on the communities in which such facilities are built, and in other communities which depend on the fruits of such expenditures. As a result of the pipeline, the growth of the state of Alaska is an example of the impact on an area as a result of the types of expenditures usually undertaken by the federal government. The Alaskan pipeline is the largest investment on the part of private industry in the history of the United States, but such scale of projects have been undertaken many times by the federal government in the form of military projects, space projects, and the huge hydroelectric projects. The impact of projects such as these undertaken by the federal government has surely been as great as that observed in the case of Alaska.

POLICY OF TAXATION

The treatment of real property and improvements of various categories under the Internal Revenue Service and its policies and interpretations has a very real and direct impact on the way in which the nation uses and improves real property. The two most apparent tax policies which influence the buyers and sellers of real property are the concept of depreciation schedules and

the provisions for tax-free exchanges or pyramiding. Both policies contribute to some degree to the tendency on the part of the
real estate industry to overbuild during periods of relative prosperity.

	1960	1975
INDIVIDUAL INCOME TAXES	44%	42.2%
CORPORATE INCOME TAXES	23.2%	13.8%
SOCIAL SECURITY TAXES AND CONTRIBUTIONS	15.9%	30.9%
EXCISE TAXES	12.6%	7.2%
CUSTOMS, ESTATE & GIFT TAXES	2.9%	3.1%
MISC. INCOME	1.3%	2.8%

Figure 9-2 *Source of Federal Revenues (by percentage).*

Source: *Statistical Abstract of the United States* (96th ed.), p. 225.

The concept of depreciation allows the owner of investment
or commercial property to write off a portion of the cost of the
improvements each year under the assumption that eventually
such improvements will have to be replaced. The important
aspect of this concept is that it is not an expense which the
owner actually had to pay. As a result, the net dollars an investor
has from the project on an annual basis is more than would be
true without the write-off of the depreciation. The actual
amount of money saved from a procedure of this kind is the
amount of taxes that would normally have been paid on such
an amount of money if it were reported as income instead of
subtracted as an expense.

The exchange concept means that if real property is traded
for another real property asset of equal or greater cost than the
adjusted sales price of the previous property, then the individual
has not incurred any tax liability in the sale and purchase. The
impact is that the gain on the first property is shifted into the
second property, and no taxes were paid on the gain so shifted.
It is important to note that such a shifting of tax liability into
the future is not a shelter from taxes or avoidance of taxes; it
merely delays the day that the taxes must be paid. What fre-

quently happens is that on the death of one of the parties, the taxes must be paid. The estate of the deceased party is billed for the taxes, and has a very limited time in which to pay such a bill. The property is then put up for sale, and often is sold at a distressed price simply to clear the estate and settle the tax liability.

The other side of the exchange concept leads to the need on the part of many investors and investor groups to constantly seek bigger and more complex projects to qualify for the tax-free exchange. In the exchange process the two properties must be the same type of property. Therefore, particularly in multifamily areas, there is a steady demand for more and larger projects to exchange, and a lessening in demand for the smaller projects. The smaller projects tend to be marketed to the young and the naive investment types. As a result the abuses in terms of misplaced properties, and very poorly managed properties, as well as marginal ownership groups, tend to dominate the small apartment house or unit group. With the passage of time, there is also a tendency for areas proliferous with small-scale apartment projects to deteriorate in terms of the quality of life and property.

Other tax areas such as investment tax credits for additions to productive capacity and various provisions for rapid depreciation, as well as a multitude of other more specific and detailed taxing policies, are at times major influences in the market of real property. The major emphasis of these programs and policies has been and continues to be the urban and industrial real estate sectors. There are similar advantages involving real property held and used for agricultural purposes; but in the main, the major impact of such policies on the part of the federal government has been in the urban areas.

STATE GOVERNMENTS

In the great majority of cases involving the direct use or improvement of real property on the part of the federal government, what actually transpires is a cooperative effort with the federal and state governments acting in partnership. In most instances, there is an aggressive competition between prospective states for the location or expansion of any large federal facility. Such competition is expressed through the political pressure exerted by the respective elected officials of each state. The opening of new military bases, as well as the closing of selective military bases, has been the scene in the past of many published debates and demonstrations of political power.

So it is with most federal projects involving large sums of money and representing potentially great economic stimulus to the locations chosen. In many instances, the states are also required to participate financially in the improvements outlined by the federal government and its agencies. Frequently the administration of such federal expenditures is the responsibility of the local office or branch of the federal agency involved, and very often represents the state and its people as much as the federal government in Washington, D.C.

	FEDERAL	STATE & LOCAL	TOTAL
1973	248 Billion	178	426
1972	223	158	382
1971	203	140	342
1970	206	128	334
1960	100	53	153
1950	44	23	67

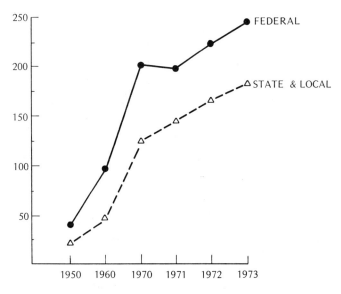

Figure 9-3 *Direct Tax Revenues*

Source: *Statistical Abstract of the United States* (96th ed.), p. 250.

HIGHWAYS

The location and building of highways is more often than not a case of matching funds on the part of the state with the funds provided by the federal government. In such cases the ability of the state to raise these funds, as well as furnish the location of such highways, becomes a very large issue in the state political scheme. The funding, location, building, and maintenance of such public facilities is often as much a state function as it is a federal function. The financing of such facilities through various bond issues or taxes directly influences the economy of the state involved. To the extent that a facility of this kind proves not to contain the spillover economic effects the state anticipated, then such a state may indeed be in for some poorer economic times as a result of such indebtedness.

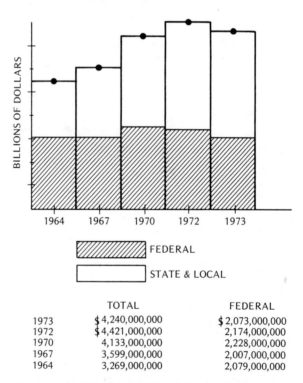

	TOTAL	FEDERAL
1973	$ 4,240,000,000	$ 2,073,000,000
1972	$ 4,421,000,000	2,174,000,000
1970	4,133,000,000	2,228,000,000
1967	3,599,000,000	2,007,000,000
1964	3,269,000,000	2,079,000,000

Figure 9-4   *Highway & Road Expenditures*

Source: *Statistical Abstract of the United States* (96th ed.), p. 564.

The funds needed for payment of interest and retiring of bonds would have to come from the state's economy. Therefore such monies would not be available for the economy of the state to use in the direct function of economic activity. It should also be kept in mind that facilities such as highways involve truly immense sums of capital. Even when the state has limited participation in raising much capital, even a small portion constitutes a very large portion of a state's capital. When some highways are costing over $1 million for each mile of road, it does not take too many miles to encounter a huge sum of capital.

EDUCATION

In most instances, education is the mutual responsibility of the state and local governments for overall educational facilities and services. The federal government provides sizable sums for educational programs, but usually these are of a very specific and specialized nature rather than the general educational programs and facilities of most states. Although the size and cost of primary education is small in relation to any one location, the overall scale of such expenditures is great. The overall quality of education is believed to be an important factor in the attraction of people and industry into a state or an area, though measurement and agreement on the standards of quality is still lacking in the public as well as the educational community.

The location of colleges and universities, however, is a major factor in the trends of urbanization and development in an urban area. Such facilities represent huge investments in facilities, and usually contain large pools of highly specialized labor and technology which attract more industry and businesses to that same area.

The orientation of the college or university in terms of areas of emphasis are vital to the character as well as the growth of such a facility. Medicine, engineering, and business have traditionally proved to be extremely fertile ground for further growth and urbanization of such communities; whereas education, liberal arts, and the vocational arts have not shown the same level of ability to attract new business and industries into an area

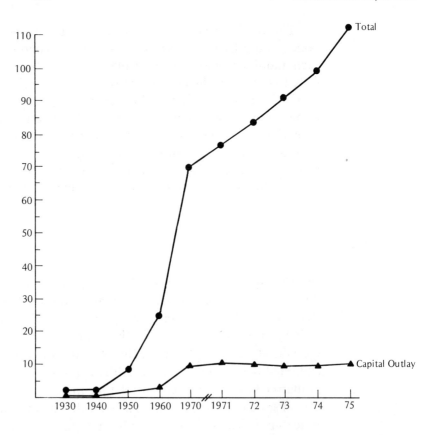

	Total Outlay	Capital Outlay
1975	$ 110,400,000,000	$ 9,700,000,000
1974	98,800,000,000	9,600,000,000
1073	89,100,000,000	8,800,000,000
1972	83,100,000,000	9,300,000,000
1971	76,700,000,000	10,000,000,000
1970	70,200,000,000	9,600,000,000
1960	24,700,000,000	4,100,000,000
1950	8,800,000,000	1,570,000,000
1940	3,200,000,000	370,000,000
1930	3,230,000,000	530,000,000

Figure 9-5   *Education Expenditures (in billions of dollars).*

Source: *Statistical Abstract of the United States* (96th ed.), p. 111.

where schools have become established. Surely there are many exceptions to these generalizations, but overall they tend to hold as valid generalizations.

COURTS AND PUBLIC ADMINISTRATION

In the early stages of economic growth of cities and towns, the location of the county seat or courthouse was a major factor in determining which city or town in a region would be the fulcrum of growth. Those cities that were not fortunate enough to attract a courthouse, very often found themselves on the backroads of growth and economic activity. With the courthouse came a multitude of other activities, and businesses which rely on the court and its record system to conduct their activities. Decisions such as to where a court should be located are therefore monumental decisions in terms of the possible impact on the land use patterns of those communities, and the rate and extent of urbanization they may come to expect.

Similarly the contemporary city and the location or expansion of court facilities have a dramatic impact on the types of activities which tend to locate in and around the area of such a facility. The major developed areas of the most intense use of land in cities of our contemporary world is mostly in and around the area in which the state and federal courts are located. In virtually every city the major financial districts are close to the local, state, or federal courthouse. The administration centers for the various state interests are also generally located near those same court facilities.

The location of such facilities is very often the result of the same process that determines the location of federal facilities. The interplay of politics and economics in the public sector is extensive and continuous, and is probably the single most influential factor—or set of factors—that tends to determine the location and size of court and administrative facilities.

STATE DEPARTMENT OF REAL ESTATE

Nearly every state has an office at the state level that is responsible for the real estate sector of the state. Most of these offices have a direct responsibility for the regulation of the industry itself. There are rules and requirements for licensing and conduct

on the part of the individuals and businesses operating in the
real estate industry. There also may be several areas of legal
regulations to protect the public in areas such as advertising, dis-
closure, fraud, misrepresentation, and a variety of other areas
related to the proper conduct on the part of the many participants in the real estate industry.

Although such state authority is usually confined to the
people who perform various functions in the market, rather than
to the product or development itself, such state authorities do
influence the performance of the market, and therefore the
factors influencing urban growth are also affected. Areas such as
legal requirements for brokers, salesmen, escrow offices, title
insurance, advertising and promotion, and the direct licensing
of such participants, are commonly overseen by state authorities.

REGIONAL AND COUNTY GOVERNMENTS

In the first instance, the county governments are usually responsible for all the unincorporated areas within a county. The
county authority is the same as the city authority in a large city,
although counties generally cover a much larger area than do
the cities. There are some areas where the city and the county
cover the same exact geographical area; but such is not the case
in every instance. As such, the county has its own planning staff,
engineering department, governing agencies, courts, law enforcement, fire protection, and virtually every area of governmental
influence that exists in large cities in developed areas. The entire
process of building permits, plans approval, inspection, and
coordination with the land use plans of the area and with the
zoning regulations, also functions in the county organization.
Therefore, in a very direct sense, the counties have indeed a
very large role in determining how and to what extent the urban
growth of the cities will influence the patterns of growth in the
county areas.

The one major area which acts as a check on the policies of
county governments is the right of people in the area to incorporate themselves into cities and towns, and thereby to
govern themselves. The costs of doing so are usually quite high
at the outset because the incorporated city or town must pay

for its own police and fire protection, its own maintenance and upkeep of public facilities, and it must elect and support financially the city administration that will replace the previous administrative body of the county. Usually the primary factor leading to incorporation is the attraction and location of some large primary industrial or commercial enterprise which can be counted on for the financial support of the new community.

The formation and role of regional agencies, in terms of economic growth and development patterns in defined economic regions, has grown a great deal during the last decade. Such agencies are generally responsible for the coordination and over-all land use planning of entire regions in various states. These agencies may include many cities and towns, and even several counties, within their area of responsibility. Their major task is the research and development of plans and impact of proposals within their areas, and to recommend or discourage the approval of such plans. The location of regional and county airports, highways, and various public works projects such as water treatment facilities, sewerage-treatment plants, recreational areas, watershed designations, and other developments have long-range impact in terms of a region's urban growth and land use.

Additionally there are many regional agencies that were formed to concentrate on one aspect or area such as coastal protection commissions, water shore commissions, mountain and ski resort protection, and many others. These agencies have a very great impact on the economies of the regions and areas involved, in addition to the impact they have on the direct land use of a subject area. Often the actions of such agencies convey the community acceptance or rejection of certain industry types or certain firms. For instance, once rejected by such an agency for a proposed hookup of sewage lines, these companies may well choose to leave that entire region. Although there would perhaps be some cities or areas of an autonomous nature that would welcome such a firm or industry, the impression left by the regional decision often remains with the firm in question.

LOCAL GOVERNMENTS

Ultimately the local government has the final say in terms of the patterns of land use within its boundaries. Cities have virtually total control over the land use decisions within their municipal boundaries. In most instances such cities and towns will support the desires of the state and federal governments in terms of land use, but the turning point usually rests on the economic advantages to the city and its citizens as a result of going along with the wishes of these authorities. The single area where this is not the case is the area of land owned outright by the federal government. Then the land may be used and improvements may be built on such land as the federal government and its agencies see fit.

Beyond facilities such as military lands and government reservations, the municipal governments have a very powerful voice in determining the land use patterns and urban growth characteristics within their boundaries. It is therefore extremely important for those concerned with local land use and the trends of growth to maintain communication and contact with the power structure in the local community. Decisions such as zoning and building regulations, open space, city transit, water, power, telephone, and other public services, business operations and licensing, economic development agencies and departments, redevelopment of older areas, schools, police, and fire protection levels, and virtually all areas of concern to the inhabitants of the land within the municipal boundaries, fall within the view and decision-making authority of the local municipal administration.

THE LEGAL SYSTEM

In discussing the subject of real property, we are discussing an entirely abstract concept. Real property, especially in the United States, is merely a bundle of rights given by and protected by a standard of law of the Constitution and the governmental system. In reality the individual property owner does not own the property so described; ownership is only of the rights to use that property in certain ways and within certain bounds. The subject of ownership is a legally defined bundle of rights. So in this way there is probably no single area of more importance in the exchange and use of real property than the legal system and enforcement processes.

In the early stages of urbanization the type of ownership of land and improvements was virtually unlimited in terms of what the owner could do on and with the subject property. As the process of urbanization progressed, and the resultant population and ownership densities increased, certain restrictions were imposed on the rights of the owner of real property to do as he or she wished with such property. This process of putting limitations and parameters around the bundle of rights so acquired in the marketplace of real property has continued into the present day. The more complex the society becomes, the more detailed and extensive such limitations tend to become. Merely the types of various estates in real property indicate the trend toward specializations in the degree of ownership acquired, and the rights associated with each type of estate differ in significant degrees.

When one adds the kaleidoscope of external limitations and requirements put on the use and ownership of real property, it is small wonder that the legal profession has become so critical to the operation of the real estate markets. As the capital requirements involved in real property purchases continue to expand, it should be expected that the continuing division of the property rights into more marketable units will also go on. As the process continues, the role of the legal profession and the role of the external factors, such as the role of governments, will likewise continue to expand.

THE ROLE OF GOVERNMENT AND LAND USE

The ownership of real property is intimately tied to the very basis of the governmental authority and structure outlined in the doctrine on which governments are founded. In the United States, the real property sector is tied directly and very closely to the constitutional rights of individuals and the rights and powers of the various levels of government; therefore the role of government—at all levels—is very important to the health and efficiency of the real estate markets, and the allocation of real estate services to the most productive ends.

Furthermore, government at all levels owns outright more than 50 percent of all the land area in the country. What the

government does or does not do with such immense land holdings substantially affects the use and patterns of urbanization
throughout the rest of the nation. It should also be noted that
in many instances, if not most, the remaining property is not all
private property in the hands of individuals. In many instances,
private nonprofit institutions own a great deal of the remaining
property. This means that in many instances less than 30 percent
of the total land in any one jurisdiction is owned by individuals.

PUBLIC LANDS	1959	1964	1969
FED	33.7%	33.8%	33.7%
STATE	4.5%	4.6%	5.0%
LOCAL	0.8%	0.8%	0;9%
TOTAL	39%	39.27%	39.6%
INDIANA LANDS	2.3	2.2	2.2
PRIVATE LAND	58.7	58.6	58.2

Figure 9-6   *Total Land Ownership.*

Source: *Statistical Abstract of the United States* (96th ed.), p. 204.

This great ownership on the part of institutions and governments means that nearly three-fourths of the land area does not
enter the normal market process. The exclusion by the majority
of the supply of land from the market tends to distort and mis-
lead a great many individuals in their analysis and conclusions
in regard to the functioning and efficiency of the free market in
real estate.

Furthermore, the burden of taxation for the largest sector of
the economy is borne by a definite minority of the total landowners in any one area. The public services which benefit all
properties in an area, such as fire, police, utilities, water, education, transportation, parks and recreation, and a multitude of
other services, are paid for and supported to the largest extent by
the remaining property owners who control and own a mere
one-third, or less, of the entire land area so served.

Although one could make a very strong case for some general
land reserve and centralized agent to control and direct the use
of such important public resources, the elevation of such an
agent or agency above the level of other citizens in terms of their
ability to measure and evaluate alternatives somehow seems a

bit distasteful to me. Urbanization, industrialization, and the development of the civilized world did not occur through the benevolent guidance and direction of some central agency of a government. It was done, and is continuing to be advanced, by millions of individuals making everyday decisions and evaluations in terms of their own best interests. Such collective results as have been seen in the history of urbanized mankind in the past 300 years would seem to testify to the efficiency of that process.

	STATE	% FEDERALLY OWNED
	ALASKA	96.4%
	NEVADA	86.5
	UTAH	66.2
HIGHEST	IDAHO	63.7
	OREGON	52.3
	WYOMING	48.0
	COLORADO	45.0
	ARIZONA	43.9
	CONNETICUT	0.3%
	IOWA	0.6%
	MAINE	0.7%
LOWEST	NEW YORK	0.8%
	RHODE ISLAND	1.1%
	KANSAS	1.3%
	NEBRASKA	1.4%
	MASSACHUSETTES	1.5%

Figure 9-7 *Federal Ownership of Land*

Source: *Statistical Abstract of the United States* (96th ed.), p. 203.

SELECTED READINGS

American Academy of Arts and Sciences, Boston. Commission on the year 2000. *The Future of the U.S. Government Toward the Year 2000.* New York: George Braziller, Inc., 1971.

Board of Governors of the Federal Reserve System. *The Federal Reserve System: Purposes and Functions.* 4th ed. Washington, D.C.: Federal Reserve System, 1961.

Meek, Paul. *Open Market Operations.* New York: Federal Reserve Bank of New York, 1969.

Moynihan, Daniel P. *Toward a National Urban Policy*. New York: Basic Books, Inc., 1970.

Roosa, Robert V. *Federal Reserve Operations in the Money and Government Securities Markets*. New York: Federal Reserve Bank of New York, 1956.

CHAPTER TEN

THE ROLE OF OTHER INSTITUTIONS

BANKING

The first major institutions that usually come to mind when one looks at the real estate sector is the whole banking industry. Banking is at the very core of the economic health of a nation or economy. Business and commerce need money in its various forms, just as we need blood in our bodies to survive. And very much like the blood in our bodies, money must be kept moving to be of much economic benefit. Money hidden under a mattress, or in a coffee can, cannot be used in commerce or trade. It cannot be used to borrow and lend, or to invest in capital improvements or manufacturing. Ultimately it ceases to become available for the payment of wages and taxes, and the entire system is hurt by the lack of use and turnover of such money as exists.

The banking industry provides the mechanism through which monies are kept employed in the economy, and through which monies are allocated to the various sectors of that economy. It should be remembered that such a money system was not fully developed until the time of the rise of the merchant class in the Middle Ages. Although there were scattered instances of money and coinage in earlier times, the widespread use of such a money system was a relatively recent development in terms of the history of the urbanization of mankind. The Industrial Revolution would certainly have been greatly retarded in its growth if no such monetary system was available. Indeed, it may have been entirely impossible.

As the banking community began to develop, its major function was to facilitate the needs of trade among the major trading nations of the time. The role of the banker was to make changes in and among various currencies found in the trading community. Also it was not long until the process of lending monies for the building of capital plant and equipment, and the joint and several ownership of such expensive items of trade as ships, and cargoes. Essentially, however, the role of banking was limited to those few people who through accumulation of wealth and assets were in a position to lend money to those sectors of the economy that needed it.

Banking as we know it today, with its emphasis on the individual consumer and the financing of consumer goods and purchases, was unknown. What really was the banking community was the merchant banking community, whose primary and sole function was to facilitate the needs and operations of the merchant and trade community.

As the trend of industrialization and urbanization spread in the different nations of the world, various forms of banking enterprises began to appear. The predominant role was that of the central bank of each country. In the British Empire it was the Bank of England, and in France it was the Bank of France. In the United States no such central banking function was performed until the creation of the Federal Reserve System in 1911. Until that time, most banks were from state charters and under state regulators. There was no national system for such state banks to shift funds from one community to another. Additionally, there was the problem of each state having its own regulations insofar as the internal operations of the banking system within the state was concerned. The comptroller of the currency was responsible for the regulation of the banks with federal charters, but such regulation was sparse, to say the least.

After the monetary crisis of 1907 brought to the attention of nearly everyone the need for some central banking facility, the Federal Reserve System was created. The role of the Federal Reserve System is essentially that of the central bank of the country. It regulates the reserve requirements, the expansion and contraction of the money supply, and the operations of the member federal reserve banks. The member banks of the Federal Reserve System are all commercial banks, and therefore the major emphasis of the Federal Reserve is on the monetary and fiscal policies of the nation. The chairman of the Federal Reserve System is an adviser to the President of the United States, and therefore has a significant input into the major economic policy decisions of the nation.

After the sour experience of the early 1930s, the need for a similar central banking function to service the savings and loan sector of the economy was abundantly clear. As a result, the Federal Home Loan Bank Board was created. The Federal Home Loan Bank (or FHLB) was the central bank of the savings and loan industry in virtually the same respects as the Federal Reserve System and the commercial banks. The central bank and the FHLB both make advances to members as necessary, as well as set the discount rates and interest rates they charge for such advances and discounts on securities. The structure of the two central banking systems is nearly identical.

There are 12 Federal Reserve banks, one in each of the 12 districts throughout the country. There also are 12 Federal Home Loan banks, one in each of the 12 districts. The districts are the same in both systems, although the location of the respective banks is in a different city in each district for the Federal Reserve and Federal Home Loan banks. Only one district has the Federal Reserve Bank and the Federal Home Loan Bank in the same city, and that is in San Francisco.

Although the central banking system of the Federal Reserve and its focus on the commercial banks of the nation is somewhat directly removed from the real estate sector, the actions on the part of that sector of the economic system are vitally important in terms of the economic growth and the subsequent urbanization of the nation. Whenever market conditions in the commercial sector deviate in a great way from similar market conditions in the savings sector, there tend to be dramatic and far-reaching results. One of the most common is the shifting of funds from one sector to the other during times of significant interest rate disparities.

DISINTERMEDIATION

The savings and loan industry is a quite regulated sector in terms of interest rates which member banks are allowed to offer. Furthermore, set interest rates tend to change much more sluggishly than the rates offered in the commercial sector. The result is that when the interest rates being offered in the commercial sector equal—and sometimes exceed—those offered in the savings industry, there may be a shifting of funds on the part of the savings account holders in the savings banks. When the owners of savings in savings and loan banks withdraw funds to invest in shorter-term notes and other instruments in the commercial sector and the Federal Reserve System itself, such shifting of funds is called disintermediation.

As a result of such conditions the available funds in the savings and loan industry are reduced, and this in turn reduces the funds available for lending to the buyers of real property. Development of real property declines; also the availability of housing usually declines. The most common remedy for such temporary conditions is raising the minimum amounts in which such commercial banking instruments may be purchased. Treasury bills and treasury notes are the most common instruments involved in disintermediations, and the pressure from the savings and loan industry is usually able to have the minimum denomination of such notes and bills raised to a minimum of $10,000. The majority of savings accounts in the industry are less than that amount, so the problem is tempered in this manner.

SAVINGS AND LOAN BANKING

The savings and loan banks in the United States were essentially very unorganized until the early 1930s. Until that time, the savings and loans operated within the charters of their respective states and did not interact with the savings and loans of other states in any meaningful way with regard to real estate. What essentially happened was that each bank was totally dependent on its own local area both for deposits and loan demand. If there were more deposits than demands for loans, the funds were not invested in other forms of real property securities. Likewise, when there was a demand for loans for building and growth in the economy of the local area beyond the amount of deposits in that same local bank, there were no facilities through which such a bank could sell its current loan portfolio in an effort to raise more capital to meet the local demand for funds. So the potential for growth in many areas was self-limiting.

The role of the Federal Home Loan Bank system was defined as one of the several agencies to help solve this problem. The Federal Housing Administration and the Federal National Mortgage Association were also created at this same time in our history. They also had, as at least one of their objectives, the creation of an active and efficient secondary mortgage market. Prior to the functioning of the secondary mortgage market, however, the role of the FHA was critical.

THE FHA

The Federal Housing Administration was created out of the depths of the depression of the 1930s. During that period, it became abundantly clear that the nation as a whole required a viable and healthy real estate sector; therefore, for the first time in our history, the federal government became directly involved in the real estate sector. Prior to that time the role of the federal government was limited primarily to the acquisition through war or purchase of real property, and the giving away of that real property in the form of homesteads and rights of way. Until that time, the intent was to develop and inhabit the land mass of the United States.

After witnessing the drastic results of the depression, it became obvious to most people at that time that the real estate sector drastically needed to become more efficient and healthy. As a result, one of the first steps was the creation of the FHA. The first role of the FHA was the establishment of some forms and standards for the real estate sector. To qualify for the great benefits of mortgage guarantees by FHA, housing had to adhere to certain standards of construction and space. Furthermore, the appraisal technology was outlined in an effort to make or create some uniformity in the underwriting practices of the various savings and loans throughout the nation.

As a result of such structuring, loans in one part of the country were regarded with some degree of confidence by other parts of the nation. A home loan issued in the state of Utah was made in accordance with the same appraisal principles and the same underwriting guide-lines as a home loan issued in New York. The additional factor of such mortgages being insured by the FHA against default made the banking community even more willing to accept such securities from banks outside the local area.

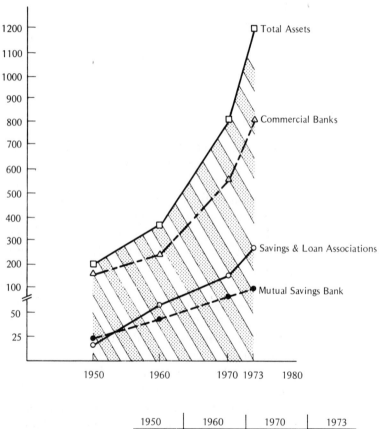

	1950	1960	1970	1973
COMMERCIAL	170.5	260.7	581.5	842.9
SAVINGS & LOANS	16.9	71.5	176.2	272.4
MUTUAL BANKS	22.4	40.6	79.2	106.7
TOTALS	209.8	372.8	836.9	1,222.0

Figure 10-1 (a) *Total Assets of Financial Institutions (in billions of dollars).*

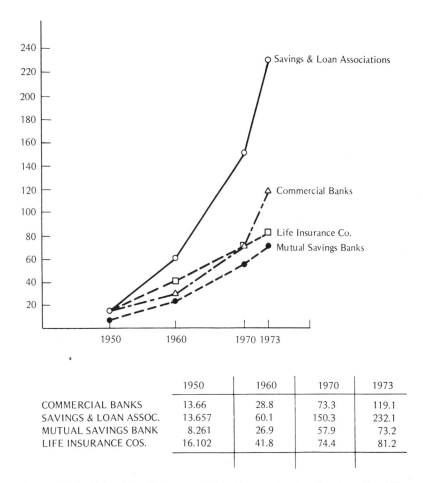

	1950	1960	1970	1973
COMMERCIAL BANKS	13.66	28.8	73.3	119.1
SAVINGS & LOAN ASSOC.	13.657	60.1	150.3	232.1
MUTUAL SAVINGS BANK	8.261	26.9	57.9	73.2
LIFE INSURANCE COS.	16.102	41.8	74.4	81.2

Figure 10-1 (b) *Total Outstanding Loans by Institution (in billions of dollars).*

The end result was that now there was some mechanism through which funds from a capital-rich area could be shifted to a capital-poor area. When the local demand for loans was below that of the deposit capacity, the subject bank could invest its excess cash in the mortgages being offered for sale by other banks. The banks in a capital-poor area where the loan demand was in excess of the available funds could now sell their existing portfolio of real estate loans, and thereby free capital with which they could now issue in the form of new loans.

Other factors such as lowered risk and lower interest rates, and

	NUMBER	ASSETS (Billions of $)
1973	14,194	$ 842.9 Billion
1970	13,705	581.5 Billion
1960	13,484	260.7 Billion
1950	14,164	170.5 Billion

Figure 10-2 *Commercial Banks*

	NUMBER	ASSETS
1973	5,200	$ 272.4 Billion
1970	5,700	176.2 Billion
1960	6,300	71.5 Billion
1950	6,000	16.9 Billion

Figure 10-3 *Savings & Loan Associations*

a new emphasis on the individual applying rather than simply the asset alone, and the extension of loans for longer periods of time with the addition of a gradual paying-off of the principal, all helped to make the real estate sector healthy again. Such instruments remain at the very center of a healthy and viable real estate sector today. The newer additions to the laws and changes in policy on the part of the state and local governments have only become more specific in dealing with more particular problem areas. The future will surely hold more changes in the roles of the various agents involved, but would seem to hold the prospect of these changes to be very limited in scope and attacking more specific and smaller problems than were true at the time such policy was formed in the early 1930s.

OTHER BANKING INSTITUTIONS

MUTAL SAVINGS BANKS

Although there are less than 500 mutual savings banks in the United States, with less than one-half the total assets of other savings banks, mutual savings banks do play an important role in those areas where they exist. The role of the savings industry is to provide secure facilities for the public and small individual accounts to deposit their savings, and also to provide funds for the residential real estate consumer. As Table 10-4 illustrates, the mutual savings banks have decreased in number nearly 10 percent between 1950 and 1973, while at the same time they have increased their total assets nearly fivefold during the same period of time.

The mutual savings banks are state chartered, and generally are not members of the Federal Home Loan Bank system. They may maintain correspondent status with that system, but usually remain within the confines of the state and local jurisdictions. Because they are local in nature, the actions on the part of the mutual savings industry with reference to a particular state are most often rather far-reaching in terms of the local economies of the communities within such states. Also, because the nature of real estate is that it tends to be a very localized commodity, the influence of local agents in the real estate industry and the banking and financing commodity is rather far-reaching in terms of the impact on the development patterns and pace of such patterns.

	NUMBER	ASSETS
1973	482	$ 106.7 Billion
1970	494	79.2 Billion
1960	515	40.6 Billion
1950	529	22.4 Billion

Figure 10-4 *Mutual Savings Banks*

As shown in Table 10-4, the mutual savings bank industry has total assets of more than $100 billion. When one recalls that such banks are generally local in character, the size of their assets offers an entirely different perspective.

	AMOUNT	% OF PERSONAL INCOME
1973	$ 180.5 Billion	20.5%
1970	127.2	18.4%
1960	56.1	16.0%
1950	21.5	10.4%

Figure 10-5 *Consumer Credit Outstanding*

	AMOUNT	% TO EDUCATION
1971	$ 1,066 Million	32%
1970	793 Million	36%
1969	677 Million	30%

Figure 10-6 *Foundation Grants*

CREDIT UNIONS

Although not considered banks in the strict sense of the word, the credit union industry is a growing one and often is an important source of capital for real property purchases as well as improvements and the durable goods which are closely associated with the level of activity in the real estate market. In the United States the credit unions have not as yet become a major lending source for the financing of real property purchases, but there are strong indications that this could become the case as that industry matures and grows. In other countries, such as Canada, credit unions constitute a major source of mortgage financing and nearly all lending in the purchase of real property is done through the credit unions.

In those communities where there may be a few major employers, and employee groups establish credit union facilities, the role of credit unions in terms of the financial structure of the community would be significantly different from the financial structure of the more metropolitan communities such as Chicago, New York, or San Francisco. Again, because real estate and urbanization is essentially a local process, the influence of such a localized financial structure as the credit unions may have a dramatic impact on how the financial community of that area complements or competes with the real estate sector.

· THE INVESTMENT COMMUNITY

When we speak of the financial needs of the nation in terms of the capital needed for the continuation of growth into the future, the entire area of financial needs in capital plant, equipment, and productive resources including real estate is the real subject. As the editors of *Business Week* magazine outlined in September of 1975, the capital requirements of the entire nation for the decade of 1975–1985 will very likely approach the $4.5 trillion level. That would be triple the amount of capital invested in the decade from 1965–1975, and nearly six times the total invested during the 1955–1965 decade.

Competing with the private sector for funds is the federal government and its various agencies. Although there is ample

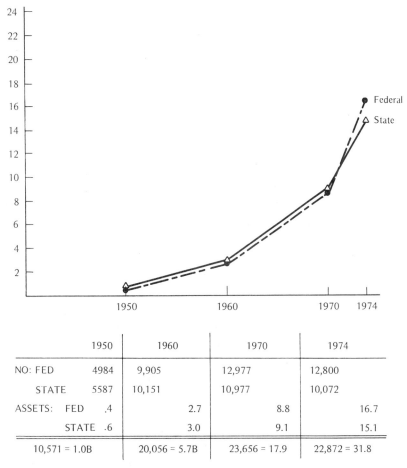

Figure 10-7 *Credit Union Assets (in billions of dollars).*

	1950	1960	1970	1974
NO: FED	4984	9,905	12,977	12,800
STATE	5587	10,151	10,977	10,072
ASSETS: FED	.4	2.7	8.8	16.7
STATE	.6	3.0	9.1	15.1
	10,571 = 1.0B	20,056 = 5.7B	23,656 = 17.9	22,872 = 31.8

cause to question the nation's capacity to generate over $4 trillion in savings and retained earnings to finance the capital needs of the private sector through 1985, when the needs of the federal government are added to that sum, especially in the light of the anticipated federal deficits, the conclusion is most surely that pressure will be added through increased demand for funds beyond the capacity of the available supply sector to accommodate. The result will tend to fall into two areas.

First, not all borrowers will be able to secure the needed capital necessary for growth and expansion. This, at the very least, will have the tendency to slow the rate of growth in the economy. Some of the nagging ills associated with the recessionary period of 1974–1975 may continue because of the retarded growth rate and recovery. Second, there will also be added pressure of an inflationary nature because of the higher cost of capital due to excessive demand. The greater demand will tend to push prices in terms of interest rates and the returns on invested capital higher than was the case in the past.

The real problem, in terms of urbanization, will most likely be continued high interest rates. Higher interest rates raise the monthly cost of occupying a dwelling. Because the interest rates will also tend to be higher during the development stage, the ultimate selling price of these additions to the housing stock will also be higher. As a result of this situation of higher prices and higher interest rates at the same time, the traditional concept of a single-family detached home for every "average" American family is quickly passing into history.

In that same article by the editors of *Business Week*, the needs of the construction industry were estimated to be nearly $2 trillion through 1985. With the terrible financial losses experienced by the real estate investment trusts, and the major banks that lent money to such trusts in the 1974–1975 recession, the ability of REITs and some major banks to lend further in the real estate sector is seriously undermined. As a result, the supply of capital to the real estate sector will probably be reduced to some extent over the near future. The impact of this supply reduction, when coupled with the added demand of the real estate sector, will tend to force development that does occur to be that of a higher-priced and more luxurious type.

EDUCATIONAL INSTITUTIONS

We have previously discussed the impact of the educational community in terms of the expenditures and capital investment such sectors represent. There is another side to the impact of the educational institutions in the nation, and that is the subjects being taught. In the case of the real estate and land use sector, it is more germane to refer to the subjects *not* being taught. In the average life of most citizens, the single largest category of expenditure, and the largest single asset in terms of personal wealth is most often real estate, and, most particularly, the ownership of a home. The average person spends more time and more energy and more money, in terms of the other portions of their lives, on the maintenance of and purchase of the family home. And yet, although more than one-third of a person's life is consumed in the home, most individuals have never taken a course in the aspects of the real estate to which they devote so large a portion of their lives.

The alternative to formal education in the principles of land use and the market forces and principles is to learn these principles through experience in the day-to-day operation of the market. The cost of such lessons learned in the street is usually very high in terms of the mistakes made in learning through experience. It is also a handicap to the community as a whole; for it is the community that must accommodate the mistakes in land use, and the patterns and gaps that tend to arise in those areas where property owners have suffered from mistakes and ultimately abandoned or neglected their property.

An example of such consumer reaction would be the large inventory of neglected homes through the FHA 235 program which plagues many communities with very high costs involved in the impact of such mistakes on those communities. Consumers with little or no knowledge in the real estate and land use areas were forced to rely too heavily on the opinions and implied judgments of federal and state officials involved in limited aspects of such programs.

The general education of the consuming public in the areas of the real estate and land use sector would in the long-run also tend to reduce the extent to which some people are forced to rely on the various segments of the real estate sector and the degree of "professionalism" that is associated with each sector. The entire subject of real estate is so very complex, and the tendency on the part of legislature is to merely compound that same complexity, that no one individual is capable of knowing all the phases of market process at any one time. Furthermore, such an education would also tend to reduce the extent to which selected professionals would be depended on to be experts in the entire area of real property.

The responsibility for complete understanding and fair

analysis should be shared by all the parties involved in the real estate sector, including the buyers and the sellers in the market. That same responsibility is shared by the public officials who propose, pass, and administer the laws and regulations in the real estate sector. Such public figures are, or should be, responsible for the passing and administering of laws applicable and understandable to all the parties in the market. The simplification and reduction of the duplication that currently exists in the real estate sector is surely in need of attention on the part of the public and its representatives.

LICENSING AND MARKETING

Largely because of the inadequate education in the consumer and public as a whole, the expectations on the part of the marketing forces and the various regulatory and licensing bodies are generally too high. There is nearly a natural abuse that takes place when poorly trained practitioners are tested and licensed to perform in an area where the majority of the principals are nearly totally ignorant. The testing and licensing required by various states is usually cursory in nature, and very often occurs at only one time in the career of most practitioners. Those who are committed to the industry frequently tend to educate themselves in spite of the general requirements rather than because of them.

The major educational pressures appear to be those generated by the professional groups within the industry itself, and not from the public at large. Furthermore, it is very often the case that to become a licensee merely requires that a passing score on some multiple choice examination (multiple guess?) is obtained. Generally there are no further educational requirements to remain in the business or industry at that level.

Another major flaw in the marketing aspects and licensing requirements is that, once licensed, an individual may practice in any phase or sector of the real estate industry that appears attractive. A beginning salesman may practice in residential, in commercial, in agricultural, in investment real estate, or virtually any sector where a person is able to generate the clients necessary to justify remaining in this field. The implication in the licensing and testing procedures is that all sectors of the real estate industry require identically the same knowledge and level of training. It would be much like saying that a general surgeon, once he passes the exam, would be qualified to practice neurosurgery or vascular surgery.

Of course the relationship when applied to the human body seems patently absurd; and yet, when applied to the major financial commitment, and the very life patterns of a nation, it is not even considered. Some of the responsibility must lie at the feet of the regulatory agencies at the state and local levels, and surely with the arms of the agencies which are responsible for the testing and licensing of practitioners in the real estate sector.

APPRAISAL INDUSTRY

Although there has been significant growth in the tools used in the appraisal of real property, there still remain some very real flaws in the approaches to the appraisal problems. The first is a common criticism that has yet to be reflected in the everyday analyses. The cost approach to appraisal is totally without merit in the analytical sense. The cost of a product does not justify a price, and therefore does not determine its value. The cost of an item deducted from the most likely selling price will determine the amount and degree of profit or loss. Value is an independent variable, and the implication that value is dependent on the cost of an item is simply to redefine value in the abstract and value judgment area of personal opinion. Such a concept of value would be totally useless in the marketplace and in arriving at the most efficient use of real property.

A second major flaw of appraising, and most particularly the appraisals with reference to valuation for tax purposes, is the assumption that if one property next door is used for an intense purpose, then there is a supportable value estimate for the subject property based on a duplication of the next-door usage. Ignoring the advantages of diversity, and the relative economies of scale in certain land use categories, the surrounding property soon becomes assessed and appraised at the same highest and best use definition.

It is this type of thinking processes which encourage the wholesale shifting of land use patterns in a community and the rapid spread or urban sprawl and strip development. The owners of such properties are very often compelled to change the use of their property merely to meet the increased demands of taxation defined in terms of the most intense use of the area. Although there is some redefinition in this area, with reference to dedicated open space or green belts for the minimum of ten years, the general appraisal community—and the lenders on real property who depend on the appraisal technicians—is still practicing appraisal on the highest and best use possible which most often translates into the highest intensity of land use possible.

PLANNING INSTITUTIONS

Although the academic discipline of planning has developed a great deal over the past 30 years, there is still a rather unknown quality about it on the part of the community and population at large. The major reason for this lack of understanding on the part of the population in general is that historically the planners had no power, but were merely advisory in their influence over the land use patterns and the shapes of the developed communities. The major flaws in the process have been the mistakes made and very well publicized, and of which the public is continually reminded and recalls having to pay for. The tremendous urban renewal projects and their expensiveness and failure are common knowledge. The recent mistakes involving rehabilitated housing, which also proved to be very expensive and nearly a complete failure in some larger cities, merely add to the general level of distrust on the part of the public for the planners in the society.

One major area of neglect on the part of the planning community, in my opinion, is the little attention paid to the economic incentives necessary for growth and change in the direction that such planners would like. The attitude that simply by planning and saying it will be, is sufficient cause to see it completed and a successful manner is too naive. And yet, many growth decisions are made on that basis. The denying of permits to build in one area is most often accompanied by the assumption that the parties will therefore build in another area.

In the past few years there has been a very large drop in the number of units being built. In many communities that drop was in a large part due to the denial of permission on the part of the regulatory agencies. The current housing shortage in the United States, and particularly in certain communities and areas, is evidence that such units were not built elsewhere when approval to build in one area was denied. The economics of a community is the primary basis for its existence, and therefore such economic causes and forces must be accounted for in the planning and land use regulation process. The study and understanding of economic principles must be a fundamental part of the academic training of the planners in the public as well as in the private sector.

TAXATION

The rationale for the taxation of real property was set in the idea that many of the public facilities supported through taxation were more to the benefit of the property owners than to those who did not own real estate. Such public facilities as fire and police protection, well maintained road and transportation facilities, and good educational facilities, are well recognized enhancements to real property values. As we have seen in the history of urbanization, many basic public facilities which caused urbanization patterns to result as they did were most beneficial to those who owned or controlled the land within the subject areas.

There has been, however, a growing tendency on the part of local governments and the various overlapping districts to look at the real property within their jurisdiction as the primary discretionary source of revenue for the general revenue needs of such bodies. There has tended, therefore, to be a growing reliance on real property owners for the financial support of various social programs such as social services, health and welfare, and a variety of other expenditure programs remotely related to real property values—if related at all. The result has been that those owning real property have seen the burden of taxation steadily increase with slight regard for the cash flow consequences of such taxes. When one encounters as much as 75 percent of the subject property of an area being held in the hands of government and other tax exempt entities, and the burden of the individual property owners comprising the remaining 25 percent of all land that must pay all the taxes, the implications are readily apparent. Taxation should complement the economic health of the community rather than cripple it. The trend of current taxing policies would seem to be moving more toward the latter, with reference to the holders of real property. New York and Detroit are not alone in terms of the problems associated with a disproportionate reliance on the real property sector as the major revenue generator for city treasuries.

CHAPTER ELEVEN

CURRENT TRENDS AND BEYOND

MIGRATION OF POPULATION

The rather large and steady migration of populations from rural areas and communities into the more densely populated urban areas has slowed to a rather dramatic extent during the past decade. Although migration shifts in the nation continue, such movements have been most dramatic in terms of the population shift from urban centers to the suburban and rural communities near the fringe of large urban centers. The implications are that the massive influx of population from rural communities to large cities has come to a rather abrupt end. The implications in terms of steadily rising tax bases is clearly illustrated by the position of New York City. Certainly not all problems of that city are the result of the slowdown in immigration, or due to the migration of wealthier segments of the population to the suburbs; but at least a portion of the financial woes of that community can be attributed to such trends.

Although the tendency to move will probably continue on the part of the population of the United States, such movement may be more specific in terms of the communities which grow and those which decline. The assumption that most rural areas will continue to lose population, and that most major cities will gain population, seems to be an assumption that has been discarded in terms of fact during the past decade. The future will surely tend to continue that same selected migration pattern.

RATE OF GROWTH

In terms of the total population of the United States, such population will tend to continue its growth through the year 2000. This is mostly a result of the fact that the majority of our population is still of a relatively young age, and therefore still in what are termed the child-bearing age group. As a result, we can rationally expect the population of the nation as a whole to continue to grow. Such growth in total population, however, will not necessarily mean a continued growth in the physical size of the urban sector of our economy. The previous trend of deserting the older sections of urban cities in favor of the new has proved to be very expensive in terms of capital investments lost in the unused older sections, and the higher costs associated with the construction of public facilities in the newer areas on the urban fringe.

It is most probable that the growth to be accommodated in the future will be a growth defined in terms of changing land use patterns in already existing urban areas. Although attempts that have been made so far have realized modest success, if any, the cost implications—both direct and indirect costs, including social and environmental costs—will tend to make such reuse of urban land areas more feasible and much more in the overall public interest.

There is current support for various policies on the local, state, and federal levels for "slow growth," "no growth," and "managed growth," and support for the prediction of a movement toward the reuse of older areas rather than the building and improving of entirely new land areas previously not subject to urbanization. Such policies also indicate that growth in urban land use patterns will tend to be very selective and inclined to vary a great deal from one community to another. The constant migration patterns of population shifts from the North and East toward the West and South in recent years show some evidence of continuing.

INFLATION

Although the exact causes of inflation are not wholly understood even by the most esteemed of economists, the impact of the inflationary trend we have witnessed over the past decade can scarcely be discounted. The impact of inflation on the real estate sector of our economy is one of major importance and consequence. Every major component included in production of improvements is affected by inflationary trends. The cost of land is often the first and most dramatically affected. The available land for development is scarce and limited in amount. Any inflationary pressure in the economy affects all items of fixed or limited supply most directly. Nearly one-third of the total cost of a single-family detached home is involved in the cost of the land and the preparation of such land for building. Inflationary pressure on land prices has an immediate impact on the feasibility of developing the land and on the final selling price of the home on completion.

Another third of the cost of building a single-family home is very often the cost of labor. Although labor costs may fluctuate more than the price of land itself, the monies involved in labor are cash outlays which cannot be financed over a 20- or 30-year period. As a result, the cost of labor as it is subject to inflationary pressure is another area of the dramatic impact of inflation.

The costs of material may approach one-fourth the cost of building a single-family home. Such costs are also subject to inflationary pressure, but may lead to substitutions of some less expensive materials for those that have risen in price due to inflation. Also, the potential for volume purchases in an attempt to reduce the costs of the material is a real alternative to the costs of construction. It remains a fact, however, that the costs of material inflated through inflation in the economy cannot be avoided altogether, and thus will tend to be reflected in the final selling price of a new home.

Finally, the inflation pressure in the economy is nearly always immediately reflected in the interest rates that lenders charge for the construction and permanent loans in the real estate sector. These costs tend to increase the selling price of the final product because of the higher charges incurred during construction. The major impact of such rises in interest costs is the increased monthly payment which the purchaser of such a dwelling will have to accommodate. As a result of the rather rigid limits in terms of monthly cost as a percentage of monthly income that banks will tend to lend to home buyers, rises in the final price and in the interest rates charged are apt to quickly price many potential home buyers out of the market entirely.

SOCIAL COSTS

The indirect costs involved in the development of real property include the environmental protection, zoning, density limits, additions to public services, dedication of large areas of land to public uses such as parks, schools, rights-of-way, utilities, streets, and a variety of other social uses. The result of such requirements is that less land area may be used for the ultimate product, although the builder had to acquire the entire land area in the first place. Additionally, such requirements extend time that vacant land must be held while plans are screened and altered and hopefully approved by numerous governmental bodies. The inspection and approval process often becomes tedious and time-consuming as it begins to involve more elements and governmental authorities. This social protection comes at a cost which must be included in the cost of producing the end product.

Although in most instances the mistakes of the past were honest mistakes, and the urban sprawl was the best alternative at the time, as a nation we must avail ourselves of the lessons learned. One of the elements of that lesson, it seems to me, has been largely ignored in the current debate over growth witnessed in many of our communities. The various proposals for improving our living areas and communities have very real and direct costs. It is totally ignorant to assume that the producer of a product will undertake all the social costs involved. He or she must earn a return for their efforts. This means that as the costs rise, so must the ultimate price of the end product. It is quickly becoming a fact that nearly every new family formation is precluded from owning a home because of the high costs. In many major urban areas the average cost of a new home is approaching $45,000. At that price level, under current financing guidelines, a family would need nearly $18,000 in order to just barely meet the minimum requirements for a loan to purchase such a home. What all this means is that in many urban areas more than 70 percent of the families cannot afford to buy a new home. Furthermore, because of the taxing formulas based on valuation, the situation is that many families cannot afford to live in the home in which they are living if they have owned it for more than five years. The plight of many older families on fixed incomes, with reference to these same rising costs of occupancy, is that they are finding themselves paying an increasingly high percentage of their total monthly income to remain in the home they have had for many years.

CONCLUSIONS

It would seem that inflation and rising costs of home ownership will be with us for a considerable part of the foreseeable future. As a result the type of home ownership that we have come to know and expect, and the methods of construction which we have nearly institutionalized in our production sector, will continue to price itself for only the most affluent. The increasing costs of needed and wanted social benefits will tend to merely add more pressure to such costs of housing.

The answer would appear to be a change in the land use concepts to allow more efficient mixture of density with open space. In addition, the introduction of new building techniques along with improved materials will hold much promise for the reducing of costs of construction. The changing in the types of structures, in the land use patterns, in the methods of construction, and in the materials employed will all have to contribute to reduction in the costs associated with the production of housing. Additionally, there simply must evolve a more cost-conscious public sector in terms of the impact of their policies and how they enforce these policies. It would appear that the last area might hold the most promise for helping to reduce the costs of production, for those are the same areas which so greatly added to the costs in the last decade.

The alternative to such change and adaption is a continuation of the current spiral of costs and prices of new housing units, in which a continuing and growing sector of our population is prevented from owning a home because of the high costs of purchase and of occupancy.

In conclusion, the uniqueness of the land use decision-making process as compared to other markets would seem to dictate that any real significant changes in the way the land is used and the patterns urban development may take in the future will come about in a very slow and methodical manner. That such changes will occur is a near certainty—if for no other reason than the changes in technology that brought about the railroad and the automobile. The impact of future changes in transportation and life styles will most surely alter the patterns of urbanization we have come to know as development in the industrialized countries. What those future patterns will be may not drastically differ from the patterns we currently observe, but they will change to accommodate human needs and demands in life style.

BIBLIOGRAPHY

Africa, Thomas W. *The Ancient World*. Boston, Mass.: Houghton Mifflin Co., 1969.

Alonso, W. *Location and Land Use*. Cambridge, Mass.: Harvard University Press, 1964.

Banfield, Ed C., and Wilson, James Q. *The Death and Life of Great American Cities*. New York: Random House, Inc., 1961.

Bartholomew, Harland. *Land Uses in American Cities*. Cambridge, Mass.: Harvard University Press, 1955.

Berry, B. J. L. *Commercial Structure and Commercial Blight*. Chicago, Ill.: University of Chicago Press, 1963.

Bosworth, Barry; Duesenberry, James S.; and Carron, Andrew S. *Capital Needs in the Seventies*. Washington, D.C.: Brookings Institution, 1975.

Bury, J. B.; Cook, S. A.; and Adcock, F. E. *The Cambridge Ancient History*. Cambridge, Mass.: Cambridge University Press, 1928.

Carter, Harold. *The Study of Urban Geography*. London: Edward Arnold Publishers, Ltd., 1972.

Clawson, Marion. *Suburban Land Conversion in the United States*. Baltimore, Md.: The Johns Hopkins University Press, 1971.

Copley International Corporation. *Consequences of Population Growth for San Diego*. San Diego, Calif.: Copley Press, 1974.

Davis, Kingsley. *Cities*. San Francisco, Calif.: W. H. Freeman & Company, 1973.

Edel, Mathew, and Rothenberg, Jerome. *Readings in Urban Economics.* New York, N.Y.: Macmillan Publishing Company, Inc., 1972.

Editorial Research Reports. "The Future of the City." Washington, D.C.: *Congressional Quarterly,* 1974.

Elias, C. E., et al. *Metropolis: Values in Conflict.* Belmont, Calif.: Wadsworth Publishing Co., 1964.

Finkler, Earl, and Peterson, David L. *Nongrowth Planning Strategies.* New York: Praeger Publishers, Inc., 1974.

Firey, Walter. *Land Use in Central Boston.* Cambridge, Mass.: Harvard University Press, 1947.

Goldsmith, Edward, et al. *Blueprint for Survival.* Boston, Mass.: Houghton Mifflin Company, 1972.

Grigsby, William G. *Housing Markets and Public Policy.* Philadelphia, Pa.: University of Pennsylvania Press, 1963.

Hamilton, Mary Agnes, and Blunt, A. W. F. *An Outline of Ancient History.* Oxford: Oxford University Press, 1974.

Hawley, Amos H. *Human Ecology.* New York, N.Y.: The Ronald Press Company, 1950.

Herzberg, Mauser, and Synderman, *The Motivation to Work.* 2nd ed. New York: John Wiley and Sons, Inc., 1959.

Hippaka, William H. *Trends in Urban Residential Development.* San Diego, Calif.: San Diego State University Press, 1960.

Hirsch, Werner Z. *Urban Economic Analysis.* New York: McGraw-Hill Book Company, 1973.

Jacobs, Jane. *The Death and Life of Great American Cities.* New York: Random House, Inc., 1961.

Jeyapalan, Nalini, and Carr, Robert A. *Impact of Institutions on Land Values.* Fresno, Calif.: California State University, 1974.

Johnson, R. J. *Urban Residential Patterns.* New York: Praeger Publishers, Inc., 1971.

Lynch, Kevin. *The Future Metropolis.* New York: George Braziller, Inc., 1961.

Makielski, S. J., Jr. *The Politics of Zoning.* New York: Columbia University Press, 1966.

Maslow, A. W. *Motivation and Personality.* New York: Harper and Brothers, 1954.

Meadows, Donnella, et al. *The Limits to Growth.* New York: Universe Books, 1972.

Mills, Edwin S. *Urban Economics.* Glenview, Ill.: Scott, Foresman and Company, 1972.

Moynihan, Daniel P. *Toward a National Urban Policy*. New York: Basic Books, Inc., 1970.

Muth, Richard. *Cities and Housing*. Chicago, Ill.: University of Chicago Press, 1969.

Netzer, Dick. *Economics and Urban Problems*. New York: Basic Books, Inc., 1974.

Park, Robert E.; Burgess, Ernest W.; and McKenzie, Roderick D. *The City*. Chicago, Ill.: University of Chicago Press, 1967.

Perloff, Harvey S., and Wingo, Lowdon, Jr. *Issues in Urban Economics*. Baltimore, Md.: The Johns Hopkins University Press, 1968.

Reid, Margaret G. *Housing and Income*. Chicago, Ill.: University of Chicago Press, 1962.

Roebuck, Janet. *The Shaping of Urban Society*. New York: Charles Scribner's Sons, 1974.

Rothenberg, Jerome. *Economic Evaluation of Urban Renewal*. Washington, D.C.: Brookings Institution, 1967.

Thompson, Wilbur R. *A Preface to Urban Economics*. Baltimore, Md.: The Johns Hopkins University Press, 1968.

Toynbee, Arnold. *Cities on the Move*. Oxford: Oxford University Press, 1970.

Turvey, Ralph. *The Economics of Real Property*. New York: Allen and Unwin, 1957.

Vroom, Victor. *Work and Motivation*. New York: John Wiley and Sons, Inc., 1964.

PRODUCTION PROCESS
OF REAL ESTATE

ECONOMIC IMPORTANCE

When we speak of the production of real estate resources, we are primarily focusing our attention on the construction industry in structures and real estate improvements. Although significant improvements are made in the agricultural sector of the economy, the major construction activity is almost solely confined to the more urban forms of government. As an indication of the size of the construction industry, and the relative size of the residential construction segment, the following table is provided.

In 1965, total construction in the United States amounted to nearly $73 billion, and residential construction amounted to nearly $28 billion. In 1972, total construction had grown to nearly $124 billion, and the residential portion of the total to nearly $54 billion. The following graph shows the relationship between the level of overall construction activity and the level of national growth as expressed in the Gross National Product (GNP). Consistently the level of construction activity has been nearly equal to 10 percent of the total economic wealth of the nation.

As such, the construction industry represents one of the

TABLE 1

Value of New Construction Annually
(in $ Millions)

Year	Total	Residential
1975	$ 130,595 million	$ 42,876 million
1974	$ 134,815 million	$ 46,769 million
1973	$ 135,456 million	$ 57,623 million
1972	$ 123,846 million	$ 54,186 million
1971	$ 109,238 million	$ 43,268 million
1970	$ 94,167 million	$ 31,864 million
1969	$ 93,368 million	$ 33,200 million
1968	$ 86,626 million	$ 30,565 million
1967	$ 77,503 million	$ 25,568 million
1965	$ 73,412 million	$ 27,934 million
1960	$ 54,632 million	$ 22,975 million
1955	$ 46,519 million	$ 21,877 million

Source: U.S. Department of Commerce, Bureau of the Census,
Statistical Abstract of the U.S., 1975, p. 702.

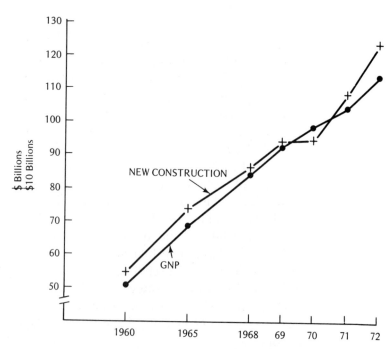

Figure A-1   *Construction vs G.N.P.—a comparison*

major segments of the entire economy of the nation. Residential construction, which is the production of housing units, constitutes a major portion of that total economic activity. When one takes time to consider all the supportive industries related to the production of real estate services, including material, maintenance, and the real estate marketing and supportive industries, the importance of the production of real estate services is immense in any measurement.

Another indication of the economic impact of the real estate production segments of the economy is the relative level of employment directly in the construction and production areas. In 1972, there were over 3.5 million people directly employed in the construction industries. With a work force of nearly 70 million people in the entire United States, real estate production accounts for nearly 5 percent of the total employment in the nation. Again, if one attempts to account for the vast number of people employed in the related industries servicing construction, the total manpower commitment in production of real estate services is immense.

Thus it can be seen why the federal government was so concerned with the construction industry during the depression years of the early 1930s, when the nation was attempting to recover from the economic basement. It is partially a result of the influence and dedication on the part of the federal and state governments to maintain a healthy and active real estate production sector that the industry and its related industries have grown to their national magnitude.

INDUSTRY CHARACTERISTICS

The construction industry, and more particularly the residential construction segment, is a highly unique industry in its structure and behavior when compared with other major industrial segments of relatively the same size. The first characteristic that comes to mind is the small size of the firms operating in the industry. When one thinks of large and complex industry, industries such as steel, automobiles, drugs, aerospace, and others come to mind. Such firms are large, highly integrated, with a great deal of centralization. For the largest, or one of the largest, industrial segments in our country, construction is typified by rather small operational units with very little concentration. The following table of construction firms by size of total sales

TABLE 2

Construction Firms by Size
(in Total & Receipts)

Class Size	Number of firms	
	1972	*1967*
0 to $24,999	499,479	482,339
$25,000 to $49,999	115,573	97,602
$50,000 to $99,999	105,641	80,429
$100,000 to $249,999	100,802	70,746
$250,000 to $499,999	45,744	30,129
$500,000 to $999,999	26,671	17,456
$1 million or more	26,896	16,137

Source: U.S., Department of Commerce, Bureau of the Census, *Statistical Abstract of the U.S., 1975*, p. 705.

illustrates this point. Over half of all the firms in the construction industry are less than $25,000 in total annual production. Of the total in construction, 83 percent reported less than $100,000 in total output during the year of observation. Figures such as these have many implications in the real estate production in the nation. The production of real estate services is extremely small-scale industry. With total sales or receipts of less than $100,000 annually, there is no capacity for large-scale technology and managerial techniques. With over half of the construction in the nation making less than $25,000 annually, there is also a high number of sole proprietors who lack the time or capacity to employ major innovative measures. Such operational scale precludes the possibility of major technological or managerial innovation originating from within the industry itself.

Since the table includes all construction firms, most of those in the higher operational levels would have to include the large government contractors who build the major federal and state projects such as dams, highways, and the largest commercial and industrial complexes. It is a rather well known characteristic of the residential construction industry that most builders are generally from the communities in which they operate.

LOCALIZATION OF THE
INDUSTRIAL UNITS

Because of the operational scale—or perhaps the reason behind it—the great proportion of residential construction firms in particular are local in their operations. By local is meant that the firms building residential structures within an economic region generally tend to originate from the same economic region. There is a distinct and extreme shortage of firms of national scale which operate in the residential construction industry. In the few that have appeared in the 1970s, several have suffered from such severe losses and lack of acceptance that many have since withdrawn from the residential construction scene on a major scale.

The small scale of operations by the majority of construction firms dictates that they will tend to be local in their operations. As a result, most firms comprising the construction industry are highly susceptible to the local fluctuations in demand for residential properties in their areas. Being local, any change in the local market characteristics tends to affect those firms more than would be the case if they had activities in other areas to emphasize in such temporary downturns.

CONSTRUCTION INDUSTRY
UNORGANIZED NATIONALLY

Partially due to the localization and resultant smaller economies of scale being performed by the residential construction industry segment, there is also very little organization within the industry itself. Most operators conduct their business on a local perspective, and very little coordination exists beyond the local level. The result is that supply and marketing data are left with vitally important influence on the operation of the construction segment in any local area. The building standards, codes, zoning, and the state of the arts in terms of management of construction companies are not developed and refined in a manner that is likely to exist in the more refined and dynamic industries of steel, autos, transportation, and many other big industrial segments of our economy.

Additional advantages that would accrue through organization, such as adequate supply of necessary raw material on a scale necessary to sustain growth within an economic area, are missing. The result is an industry that may be the innocent victim of economic fluctuations, rather than a dynamic force in the elevation of some of the ill effects of economic fluctuations and temporary maladjustments in the supply and demand accommodations within the marketplace. With a product as universally held and as economically significant as real estate, lack of such organization within the marketplace will surely be a focal point of concern on the part of academicians and leaders in the national scene of real estate in the future.

The lack of organization and the small economies of scale practiced in the real estate sector substantially contribute to the cyclical over- and underbuilding that occur in the industry. Table 3 and more particularly the graph following it (Figure A-2), illustrate this fluctuation and cyclical pattern in the housing starts or production of housing in the United States. When one begins to examine local building patterns, these cyclical trends tend to

TABLE 3

New Housing Starts, 1960 to 1975

Year	Number of Units
1975	1,126,000
1974	1,352,000
1973	2,058,000
1972	2,379,000
1971	2,085,000
1970	1,469,000
1969	1,500,000
1968	1,546,000
1967	1,322,000
1966	1,196,000
1965	1,510,000
1964	1,561,000
1963	1,642,000
1962	1,492,000
1961	1,365,000
1960	1,296,000

Source: U.S., Department of Commerce, Bureau of the Census, *Statistical Abstract of the U.S., 1975*, p. 683.

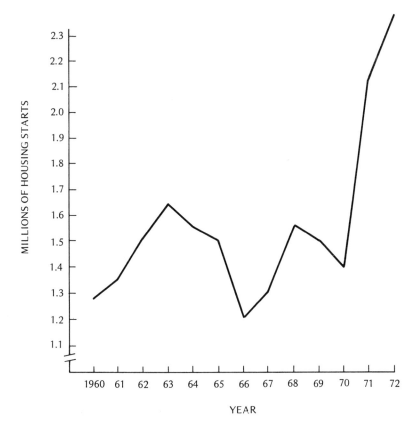

Figure A-2

become magnified. In local areas, sometimes there are extended periods of construction of new housing as a result of sustained growth through immigration. Trends such as these have been noticeable in the far western and the southeastern parts of the nation for the last several years. As a footnote to the table cited, current indications are that the 1973 statistics have fallen below the levels of 1972 and 1971.

On a local level, the cyclical characteristics of the construction area are more defined than on a national scale. Generally when there is a built-up demand for housing, and there is also available monies with which to finance the construction process, then local firms enter the residential construction market. Since most often they are small and local, these firms do not have significant research departments; they tend to follow one another on the basis of whether they possess the skills and manpower to do the job, and if they can obtain the construction financing to go through with it. As a result, they all try to complete their projects within a short time of one another. The usual outcome is a temporary oversupply of units that takes the market a while to absorb. There is a slowdown in construction until the empty units are sold and the market recovers. The following figure illustrates this tendency in a descriptive sense.

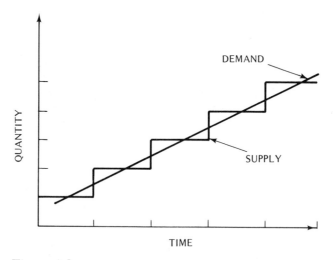

Figure A-3

With a fairly steadily rising demand for housing in an area, the supply characteristics are generally inclined to move in stepladder fashion. The result is the alternate excess, and then shortage.

THE "RATCHET EFFECT"

The staircase trend of supply in relation to the demand for real estate services, particularly urban land use services, also tends to reflect some of the fundamental factors associated with real estate. Because of the very uniqueness of real estate goods being exchanged, that market of such goods also behaves a bit unlike most other commodity or service markets. The long-term considerations involved in the production of real estate goods tend to make real estate highly inflexible in the market. This is particularly true in the circumstances of a sudden and prolonged market depression or decline.

In the situation of a falling market, the supply of real estate services is not normally capable of reducing in the normal manner. The only force of reduction is the deterioration of the physical real estate resources. Because of the trends of real estate in construction, such a market decline is likely to produce a reduced supply of real estate services in sudden drops due to deterioration of the structures from long neglect because of abandonment.

The general trend of groups of structures to be built around the same period would correlate with similar groups of structures falling out of the market through deterioration at rather sudden points during such a long-term market decline. The inability of the real estate market to adjust downward, on the supply side, to sudden drops in the demand for structure gives rise to the description of the nature of the market adjustment processes as a ratchet.

ECONOMIC IMPACT OF INDUSTRY CHARACTERISTICS

At the beginning of the current chapter we reviewed the economic significance of the residential and general real estate construction industry in terms of the national economy. Accounting for nearly 10 percent of the national output annually in direct terms, and surely much more than that in terms of the auxiliary industries supporting the construction and maintenance efforts in real estate, the production process in real estate is at the very foundation of our economic well-being. Therefore, even the slightest of imperfections or distortions in the industry have a dramatic impact on the welfare of the entire nation.

It has been estimated that a 1 percent reduction in the cost of housing, either in purchase or maintenance, would result in a total saving of $1 billion on the national level (Kaiser Commission, p. 114). So the economic impact of the industry characteristics is indeed a large task to which to address ourselves. The following discussion will confine itself to the characteristics we have described so far, and some of the major consequences of such characteristics.

SMALL ECONOMIES OF SCALE

The size of the firms operating within the major segment of the real estate construction industry are unusually small for so large an industry. Nearly 85 percent of the firms in the industry are less than $100,000 in total annual receipts. As a result of such small size, most of the construction firms operate on a nearly marginal level with very little capital investment, and often many enter and leave the industry. The result is a lack of stability within the market itself, and instability contributes to the lack of capital investment and economies of scale that may be possible.

Additionally, the small size of most firms within the industry tends to rule out the capacity for extensive innovation within the residential construction industry in particular and the construction industry in general. On the scale that most construction operates, the profit-saving advantages of most innovation techniques would not substantially change the below-the-line profits of the typical firm. As a result, the motivation for change and innovation, particularly if it entails substantial investment capital, is missing from the largest segment in the construction industry.

LOCAL NATURE OF CONSTRUCTION FIRMS

The fact that the majority of firms engaged in the production of real estate improvements are local in origin has a dramatic impact on the nature of the industry. The first element is the high susceptibility to market fluctuations. Although the national real estate trends tend to be rather steady in their trends over the five-year periods, in most cases the impact on local areas is dramatically different in nature and in the extent of the movement within the common real estate cycles that persist. Housing starts may increase by 10 percent nationally; but a given local area may incur substantial construction declines due to the many market factors that may affect one market more than another.

Thus a local firm might be much more subject to these local variations than would a national firm. The national firm may have the capacity to shift resources and material from one temporarily slowed-down local market to another local market experiencing a significant rise in construction activity.

A second element relating to the local nature of the construction industry is that being local, such firms are much more subject to the local political and financial forces and capacities of an area. Factors such as material supply, labor, financing for construction, planning and building permits and codes, tend to magnify the vulnerability of the firm that is local in nature and capacity. The ability to attract capital from outside sources greatly enhances the ability of the contractor to negotiate a fair rate of interest as well as adequate amounts of capital to facilitate his project. In addition, material and labor in key areas may be a premium that would allow a firm to complete a project which another firm without access to such national markets would be unable to complete at a feasible cost.

LOCAL BUILDING CODES PREVENT NATIONAL STANDARDS

In the economic sense, the unorganized nature of the production process in real estate is most dramatic in the building codes and zoning regulations which exist in nearly every locality. These regulations are municipal in their nature and may vary to nearly infinite extremes between localities. The result of such parameters is a physical impossibility to build units in a manner so as to abide by all the regulations of all the cities and counties in all our fifty states. Such requirements are inclined to enforce the prevailing tendency for construction firms to be local in their origin and small-scale in their operations. The result is lower operating economies subject to greater frequencies of fluctuations, and a higher cost to the builders, owners, and consumers of real property services.

OPERATION BREAKTHROUGH

Indeed, the characteristics in the production process of real estate services were so contrary to what most people felt was the efficient way to produce improvements, that the federal government entered the picture through the United States Department of Housing and Urban Development (HUD) after its formation in 1965. At that time, HUD found the constraints in the production of adequate housing for the citizens to be:

1. A fragmented housing market.
2. Restrictive building and zoning codes.
3. Shortages and inefficiency of skilled labor.
4. Processing red tape.
5. Poor use of land.
6. Restrictive labor practices.
7. Inadequate management methods.
8. Absence of adequate short-term and long-term financing.

In an attempt to overcome some of those industry shortcomings, several research and experimental programs were started. Primarily they were aimed at the more technical nature of the industry problems. Concepts such as manufactured housing and modular units constructed off-site—to be later assembled on-site —and various other technical aspects of the production problem, were addressed in the federal program. In 1970, 73 contracts were awarded in the HUD experiment for a total of $27 million. In the following year, there were 65 contracts for a total of nearly $26 million.

As a result of these and many other research projects relating to the real estate and construction area, significant advancement has been made in the areas of design and material improvements in the construction of housing units. Although in some cases the acceptance of a new method or process has been slow, the industry and the ultimate consumers of technological advancement have benefited from some of the real progress made during the past 10 years. Technology has actually not been our major obstacle to advancement in solving some of our major social problems. We have the industrial capacity to construct, and the technical skills to design entire cities in single buildings or structures compatible with our environment and enriching the lives of those who inhabit them.

Our major problem is in being human beings and either blessed or cursed with that capacity of will and individual direction which may enrich the life of the individual, and coincidentally hamper progress on the group or species level. Individualism in the production processes of real estate correlates very highly with the fractionalism of property ownership in the land use planning and patterns that develop. We have come to the conclusion that zoning regulations are necessary to overcome some of the disadvantages of fractionalization of ownership. When one observes the major problem areas identified with the production process in real estate, one can see many similarities with the justifications for zoning in land use.

CURRENT PROBLEM AREA IN THE PRODUCTION PROCESS

Many of the earlier mentioned constraints found by HUD are currently seen on the construction scene. The housing market in aggregate is by its very nature severely fragmented. This fragmentation persists into the contemporary market. Although a few large and planned communities are beginning to appear, the majority of housing starts are still spread out among the major cities in the nation. In addition, even within one major city or area the housing starts are not concentrated in one area but are spread out in various areas throughout the major metropolitan areas and their fringe areas. As a result, there is very little promise in the future of entirely alleviating the fragmentary nature of the housing production industry.

Some centralization and concentration will increase as the new planned communities increase in number and size, but the current population trends dictate that this will be short-lived as our population begins to stabilize. Some additional concentration may occur in the rebuilding efforts being introduced in the larger major cities. The migration of major population segments back into the central cities, and their rejuvenation, may lead to lessening of such fragmentation. It is, however, also a short-lived promise, and would not permanently alleviate the fragmented character of the production sector of the real estate industry.

The presence of extensive "red tape" in processing production commitments, and the actual exchange in the marketplace, is an area of increasing and growing magnitude. With the growth of environmental considerations, and the "social advantages and disadvantages" associated with given proposed projects as a required part of the preconstruction process, the future does not hold bright promise for any substantial reduction in the processing time required in the production process. In part, the extensive planning and processing steps prior to actual construction are reflective of the very nature of the real estate commodity itself.

Referring to the classes of estates in real property, and the technicalities involved in the ownership of real property, much of the red tape is more reflective of the product itself than of the various social and government requirements relating to it. Through some consolidation on the part of government agencies regulating the various aspects of real property use and transfer, there is the prospect of some reduction in the processing times associated with improving real property. The impetus for such improvement, however, appears to be directed at the governmental sector rather than the private sector involved in real estate production and improvement.

With respect to the poor use of land, the rising costs of real estate services and real property will tend to direct nearly all national attention to the efficient growth pressure from the major population centers. To the extent that such poor land use is the function of outdated and shortsighted planning and zoning regulations, the economic pressures placed on the major population segments of our nation, and to some extent the world, will force such changes in those regulations because of economic pressures.

Improved planning on the part of municipal planning agencies and with the coordination implied in the regional planning concept, some of the shortcomings resulting from the fractionalization of ownership and competing municipal interests should be overcome. The result should be more improved land use within regions for the benefit of all the population segments within the regions concerned. The one major flaw in such analysis is the planning function itself. As the following figure illustrates, the planning departments of most municipalities have an advisory function only. In most municipal organizations, the planning department is staffed by well trained and experienced urban planners. That department is within the city administration. In proposed projects the planning department researches the possible impact of the projects, and makes a professional recommendation to the planning commission on whether the project should be approved or disapproved in light of the land use plans of the city. Generally the planning commission is composed of a wide variety of public citizens without extensive economic or planning knowledge. The commission then makes its decision, based on the planning department's analysis and recommendation and on the personal beliefs of the commission members.

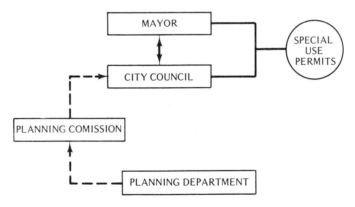

Figure A-4

If the project is refused a permit, the principals may appeal to the city council which is composed of elected representatives of the public rather than the appointed members who sit on the planning commission. If such procedures are negative, there is still one more avenue the principals can take. Through a procedure known as a special use permit, or a variance permit, the developers may circumvent the entire procedure. Since the mayor and the city council are most often politicians, they tend to be subject to political pressure if it originates from the proper sources and is intense enough to provoke action. The special use permits are most often associated with very large projects planned by very important people on the local political scene. Through the issuance of a special use permit, the entire land use plan of an area may be contradicted. It is in these ways that the best plans for a region or municipality may be totally ignored in the actual patterns of land use that develop. Until the persons with the expertise in economics and urban planning inherit some power or authority to enforce their planning decisions, the instances of poor land use relative to the total good of the community and its citizens will continue to reappear.

PROBLEM AREAS LIKELY TO BE SOLVED

The four problem areas likely to hold promise of solution in the future of real estate are: 1) Restrictive building and zoning codes; 2) the shortages and inefficient use of skilled labor that tends to characterize the industry; 3) the restrictive labor practices; and 4) the general absence of short-term and long-term financing. The reasons for promise in these areas as opposed to the other areas is that they tend to be more specific in the nature of the problem concerned. Where the previous problems may be indicative of the very nature of the real estate product and the basic nature of the market process of supply and demand, the four topics mentioned above are more reflective of specific practices of those operating within the market for real estate services and their production capabilities.

Restrictive building codes tend to be fairly common in the municipal jurisdictions which have formal building codes that date much before the 1960s. Rather than specifying from what materials a building and its parts must be built, a rewording of the codes in terms of what objectives are to be reached or maintained would be likely to open the area to innovation in technical materials and handling beyond what now exists. The rewriting of building codes could also be stimulated from the governmental level with very little procedural problems.

The cooperation of the various elements of the industry that possess an inappropriate advantage due to the requirements of such codes would be the largest single obstacle for such an effort on the part of local or regional governmental bodies. Specific state or federal governmental influence or pressure could substantially reduce resistance to such a rewriting to the benefit of the majority of the citizenry of the areas involved. The restrictive zoning codes present another more complex issue. Both areas are totally within the jurisdiction of local municipalities, and could not be unilaterally removed or modified by the federal or state governments. The major impetus for changes will probably be in the area of certain economic incentives originating from the state or federal level to promote changes for the benefit of regional planning and improvement.

So long as certain groups are the recipients of distinct economic advantages that would not—or that they believe would not—persist if such changes were made, then changes will tend not to be made. But if the economic returns to the region of the major elements of a region, or the real estate production industry within a region, outweigh the economic strength of the specific groups, then changes in building and zoning codes will tend to succeed. Because of the move toward regional planning agencies at the impetus of the federal government, there is a very real hope that the restrictive zoning codes will tend to be modified in the best interests of the citizens of all the regions concerned.

The problem of shortages and inefficient use of skilled labor is a major problem in the industry as a whole. Many of these problems are the result of the small economies of scale of the majority of firms operating within the industry. It is possible that as the size and scope of firms operating within the industry grow, much of this problem will be addressed. It remains, however, for the industry to restructure itself and provide the necessary opportunity for firms of a national scope to enter the market. With a firm of national scale, certain economies of scale would become available and labor could be employed on a more permanent scale. As the size of projects grow materially and financially, there is hope that such incentives will begin to appear in the industry sufficient to attract internal structural changes.

The problem of restrictive labor practices became most apparent when operation breakthrough attempted to introduce the manufacturing techniques of major industry to the construction industry. Through manufacturing units in a centralized location and facility of substantial size, large cost savings could be realized. Material might be purchased on a bulk scale, and the division of labor could be achieved.

It was the division of labor that led to many if not most of the problems in adapting these techniques to the industry at large. It was not necessary to employ journeyman carpenters and plumbers and electricians when producing housing units on the assembly line basis, where each station in the line performed only one task of a relatively simple and/or routine nature. Where a journeyman carpenter, for instance, is required to be proficient at building forms for cement, floors and wall studs and framing, hanging doors and windows, and doing finish cabinet work, the tasks performed on the assembly line would involve many more people each doing only one part. The resultant lower skills required would not necessarily justify the wages earned by the person capable of performing all tasks.

Through the strong organization of the skilled trades labor force, such displacement of their members with less skilled and lower-paid personnel was and is a major issue. The trend toward subcontracting for framing off-site, and buying premade cabinets at an off-site location, tends to give promise that innovations of this kind are in fact creeping into the production process in real estate. The economic benefits to be derived by the producers and consumers of real estate buildings are such that continued division of labor seems assured. The stability of the labor force in the specialized areas is also an attraction to those composing the skilled trades in the construction industry. Improved cooperation between organized labor and governmental interests could significantly advance such trends to the benefit of the majority if not all in the industry.

The last major problem area of an absence of adequate short- and long-term financing in the production process is a continual problem throughout the entire real estate sector of our economy. It is not only a problem in the production process, but a continual problem in the marketing area of real estate. The following graph reflects the fundamental problem involved in the financing of real estate. Banks and major financial institutions raise capital through various short-term accounts. These short-term accounts are the borrowed funds for such institutions. Being short-term in nature, they fluctuate according to the current economic conditions prevailing in the money and financial markets. The funds generated through such accounts, however, are funds used to finance the long-lived real estate interests. Generally these real estate interests are long-term loans of one form or another. Since the loans are relatively fixed in the amounts they will return to the financial institutions, and the short-term accounts are forever fluctuating, the result is an alternate profit and loss depending on the spread between the two.

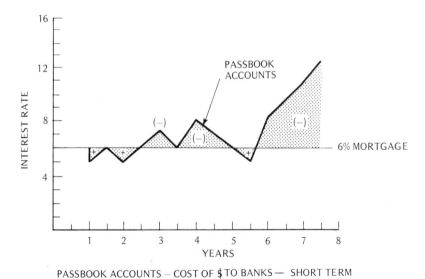

PASSBOOK ACCOUNTS – COST OF $ TO BANKS – SHORT TERM
MORTGAGES – PRICE OF PRODUCTS = PROFIT – LONG TERMS

Figure A-5

DISINTERMEDIATION

When the returns capable of being earned in the short-term interest accounts are substantially below the returns promised

in other forms of investments, there is a shifting from the lower
to the higher returns. This involves the withdrawal of funds
from the savings type institutions and the reinvestment of such
funds in other areas. Generally these other areas are not real
estate oriented. The result is a decrease in the amount of funds
available for real estate financing. The flow of funds out of the
savings institutions into other higher yielding investments on a
short-term basis is called disintermediation.

Because of the nature of the real estate industry and the
financial industry that interacts with it, the consequences of
fluctuations are severe in terms of productivity level and the
economies of scale to be realized through more stability. Lack
of such funds in the real estate sector has a rather immediate
impact on the production of real estate improvements, and also
on the marketing of units already completed or offered for re-
sale. There is the capacity on the part of the nation to substantially alleviate some of the more severe of the consequences of
such fluctuations in the money markets.

One solution has been to advocate the variable rate mortgage. The effect would be to tend to make the rate of return
earned on the part of financial institutions on their mortgages
follow the pattern of the short-term passbook accounts which
represent the cost of borrowed capital to the same institutions.
The fundamental problem of borrowing short-term and lending
long-term could be addressed by making the loans subject to
the short-term fluctuations. The result would be costs based on
the short-term and profits keyed to the same short-term conditions.

The other fundamental solution would be to finance real
estate loans with capital raised in the long-term market. Through
the issuance of long-term bonds bearing a fixed interest rate, the
proceeds from the same bonds could be used to finance long-
term real estate mortgages at a fixed spread above the costs of
the bonds. The ultimate impact of this approach would be to
loan money in the long-term from the funds borrowed in the
same long-term time frame. It is obvious that something must
be done—hopefully in the near future—to equate the time parameters of the debt market largely supportive of the real estate
industry.

The continued fluctuation between feast and famine, mostly

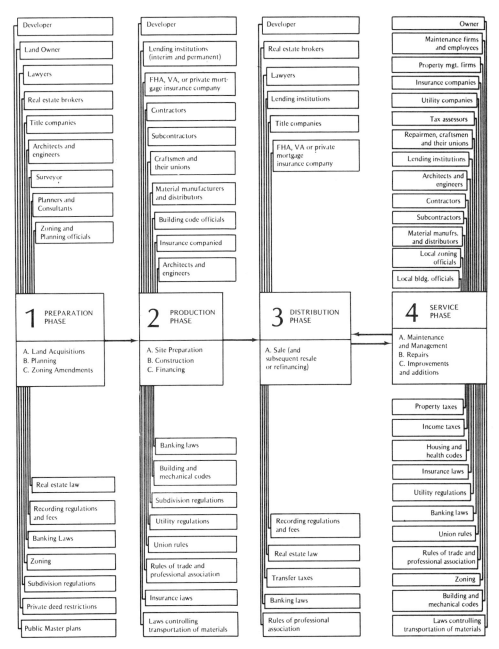

Figure A-6

Source: U.S. Commission on Housing, *A Decent Home,* 1968 (United States Printing Office) p. 115.

famine in the inflationary market, that has plagued the whole of the real estate production process, and the financing complexities which evolved in the financing involved in the marketing segments of the whole real estate industry, cannot continue to be tolerated indefinitely. It would also appear that the role of the federal and state governments could be significantly expanded in this particular area. The capacity for such an innovation on the part of the private sector would seem to be far below that necessary to substantially solve the short-term versus long-term problem and its manifestations on the national real estate level.

INDEX